PARADE AND PROTEST

A Discussion of Parading Disputes in Northern Ireland

by

Neil Jarman and Dominic Bryan

Centre for the Study of Conflict
University of Ulster

Parades and Protest
A Discussion of Parading Disputes
in Northern Ireland
by
Neil Jarman and Dominic Bryan

Centre for the Study of Conflict
University of Ulster at Coleraine

ISBN 1 85923 048 2

1996 Centre for the Study of Conflict

ACKNOWLEDGEMENTS

We are indebted to a wide range of institutions, interest groups and individuals with whom we have had frank discussions during the compilation of this report. Whilst not everyone will find it easy to agree with everything we have written we hope that their views are fairly reflected at some point in this work. The interpretations are, of course, our own responsibility.

This research was only made possible thanks to the constant support and guidance from Professor Seamus Dunn and Professor Tom Fraser of the Centre for the Study of Conflict. Special thanks is also due to Ruth McIlwaine for her patience and time, and for her skill in preparing the manuscript for the printers.

Whilst CCRU assisted this project financially, it does not necessarily endorse the views expressed in this report.

Foreword

It is clear that the practice of marching and parading in Northern Ireland is a way of confirming and reinforcing self-esteem; a continuing public manifestation of the insecurities and uncertainties of its two communities. In recent years these marches have become a sort of proxy for the violence and battles of the very recent past, and the danger that we all fear is that they will also act as a prelude to a new period of communal strife.

It is surprising, however, how little has been written about them, given their central and entrenched place in the annual life of the region. It is therefore with particular pleasure that the Centre for the Study of Conflict now publishes this original and most illuminating analysis and discussion of parades in Northern Ireland. The two authors have studied the phenomenon at first hand as they are assiduous attenders at parades, and have discussed their meaning and significance with all interested and all involved parties. They have produced - perhaps for the first time - a clear analysis of how many parades take place, where and when they take place, and the range of organisations involved in organising them. They have tried to understand how these organisations liaise with each other, and how the whole annual programme is managed, administered and formed by tradition.

Finally they have made a clear and provoking analysis of the possible approaches to resolving the dangers and difficulties which parades sometimes present, with special reference to the conflict between the right to parade and the right to live without provocation.

Seamus Dunn
May 1996

PREFACE - MARCHING THROUGH 1996

This study was written between January and March 1996 as the new marching season drew near. Interviews and conversations with parade organisers, bandsmen, residents groups, the police and those involved in promoting mediation or cross community dialogue, indicated that little, or no, progress had been made since the autumn of 1995. There appeared to have been little contact between any of the opposing parties since the previous summer, and in most cases there seemed to be little in the way of either hope or expectation that dialogue would move the debate forward. There was no public talk of compromise, if anything positions had hardened. Individuals and groups seemed to be digging in for another summer of 'angry voices and marching feet'.

On Easter Monday 1996 there was a fourteen hour stand-off at the Ormeau Bridge, after the local Apprentice Boys club had been banned from parading along the lower Ormeau Road. The attacks on the police by a small section of the crowd protesting the ban were at least as violent as at any similar confrontation last year. The responses were largely predictable. The media expressed outrage. The parade organisers disclaimed responsibility for what happened. Politicians wrung their hands. Some blamed the 'hangers-on', others appealed for calm, for dialogue, for compromise. The story remained prominent for a few days and then quietly disappeared.

The problem of contested parades will not go away simply by ignoring it. The riot at the Ormeau Bridge did not mark the beginning of this year's marching season. The first contested parade was held on 3 March in Lurgan. Nationalists wanted to hold a rally in the town centre on a Sunday afternoon. Loyalists protested and the RUC restricted the parade to one end of the town. The march and rally passed off peacefully but a massive police presence was maintained. In response to the police ban, nationalists have protested at two band parades in Lurgan which both passed through the Wakehurst estate. This was once a loyalist area but is now largely nationalist. To their credit the bandsmen did reach a compromise with the police. They restricted their parade through the estate to three local bands and they also provided more comprehensive stewarding through the town centre than at many similar events. However, the Nationalist Right to March group still question why they continue to be excluded from the town centre on a Sunday afternoon while loyalist parades are allowed through nationalist areas. And why loyalist parades are permitted to occupy the town centre two weekends in a row.

Apart from the ongoing dispute in Lurgan, there have also been clashes following a band parade at Crossgar on 19 April; another stand-off on the Ormeau Road after the Orange parade to the Orange Widows service in the Ulster Hall, on 28 April, was re-routed; and a controversial Apprentice Boys church parade in the nationalist town of Dunloy in County Antrim on 19 May.

Not all has been negative, however. Compromises were made by bandsmen in Lurgan. Following the disturbances at Crossgar, it was reported in the press that local bandsmen met with the police to ensure similar events did not occur in the future. The band parade in Castlederg (27 April), which ended in violence last year, passed off peacefully this year. Sinn Fein voluntarily re-routed their Hunger Strike Commemoration parade (5 May) away from both the Suffolk estate and Donegall Pass. The Ballynafeigh District centenary parade (8 May) passed off quietly and with a minimum of policing.

Nevertheless, there are still many parades that will provoke objections and protests in the forthcoming months. Some of these will involve a return to the disputes of last year, Bellaghy, Derry, Portadown, Dunloy, and Rosslea have all made the news already. Other protests will be made at parades that occur on a non-annual basis.

The variable nature of the disputes suggest that the issue will only be resolved through a mixture of local compromises and some recognition of wider principles about rights to parade and rights not to suffer parades. Nevertheless, there has been little in the way of sustained discussion about the way to move the issue forward. A range of individuals have suggested that an independent tribunal may have some value. Church of Ireland Primate Robin Eames, the RUC Chief Constable Sir Hugh Annesley, the Alliance Party, Mary Harney, leader of the Progressive Democrats, the Lower Ormeau Concerned Community group and the SDLP have all expressed some form of interest in the proposal since Marjorie Mowlam, the Labour Party Shadow Northern Ireland Secretary, first mentioned the issue this year. However, as the study indicates, an independent body was suggested by Sinn Fein's Barry McElduff in May last year. It was also suggested by the then Chief Constable of the RUC, Jack Hermon, in 1986. In ten years things have not moved very far. The idea of an independent tribunal has received no support from Unionist politicians, but they have offered little in the way of alternatives.

At the time of writing, in early May, the idea of a tribunal has not progressed much beyond the realm of a sound bite. There has been little in the way of serious discussion about what it might involve, how it might be introduced and what sort of problems need to be overcome. Besides the tribunal, the only recurring idea is for parade organisers to be more responsible for the totality of events and individuals involved in the parades they organise. Again there has not been any elaboration as to what this might entail in practice.

This document has been produced with three aims. First to provide some of the background to the organisational structure of the parade organisers, why they organise parades and when. Second to review the events of last year, to suggest some of the complexities and interconnections of those events and to review the attempts that were made to resolve the issue. Finally to review some of the attitudes to parades and the ideas that have been expressed to us about possible ways forward. It is not a blueprint for resolving the issue of the right to parade, but it does offer a range of possibilities for debate.

Neil Jarman, Dominic Bryan.
May 1996.

CONTENTS

INTRODUCTION	1
PART ONE - PARADES, AN OVERVIEW	4
Section One - Parades, An Overview	4
Section Two - Loyalist Parading Organisations	6
2.1 The Orange Institution	6
2.2 The Royal Black Institution	10
2.3 The Apprentice Boys of Derry	11
2.4 The Bands	12
2.5 Other Parading Bodies	13
Section Three - Varieties of Parades	15
3.1 Main Commemorative Parades	15
3.2 Local Parades	18
3.3 Feeder Parades	19
3.4 Church Parades	20
3.5 Arch, Banner and Hall Parades	21
3.6 Social Parades	22
3.7 Occasional Parades	22
3.8 Competitive Band Parades	22
3.9 Commemorative Band Parades	23
Section Four - An Average Parading Year	25
4.1 Chronology of the Main Parades	26
4.2 Local Variations	29
4.3 Band Parading Practices	31
Section Five - Overview of Parades, 1985-95	35
5.1 Ten Year Overview	35
5.2 Growth in Parade Numbers	37
5.3 Republican Parades	39
5.4 Summary	40
PART TWO - PARADES IN CONFLICT, 1995	42
Section Six - Build up to the Parades Dispute	42
6.1 Background to the Ormeau Dispute	43
6.2 Easter, the Marching Season Begins	45
6.3 VE Day and other Belfast Parades	47
6.4 Disputes in Castlederg	50
6.5 Summary	51
6.6 Possible Ways Forward	53
Section Seven - The Orange Marches	55
7.1 From Belfast to Bellaghy and Back	55
7.2 The Siege of Drumcree	61

	7.3 Agreement on the Ormeau?	63
	7.4 Arson and Vandalism	67
	7.5 Summary	68

Section Eight - Lurgan and Derry 70
    8.1 Sinn Fein in Lurgan 70
    8.2 Walking Derry's Walls 71
    8.3 Protests Elsewhere on the August Twelfth 76
    8.4 Summary 77

Section Nine - The Black Parades 79
    9.1 Black on the Ormeau 79
    9.2 Provincial Protests 80
    9.3 The Season Draws to a Close 82
    9.4 Summary 83

Section Ten - Overview of the Disputed Parades 85
    10.1 Typology of the Disputed Parades 85
    10.2 Compulsory and Voluntary Re-routing 88
    10.3 Locating the Disputes 90

PART THREE - PROBLEMS AND RESOLUTIONS 94

Section Eleven - Attitudes and Perceptions to Parades 94
    11.1 The Importance of Parades and why so many? 94
    11.2 Why are Loyalist Parades Opposed? 98
    11.3 Support for Loyalist Parades in Disputed Areas 103
    11.4 The Police and Policing 108
    11.5 The Media 111
    11.6 Conclusions 112

Section Twelve - Resolutions? 114
    12.1 Negotiation and Mediation 115
    12.2 Guidelines for Parades 118
    12.3 A Parading Commission 120
    12.4 Use of the Law 122
    12.5 Responsible Parading 123
    12.6 A Parading Tribunal 128
    12.7 Parade 'Planning' Permission 132
    12.8 Conclusions 136

PART FOUR - REVIEW 137

Section Thirteen - The Disputed Areas 137

Section Fourteen - Review of Main Issues 144

References 150

INTRODUCTION

It was hoped that the summer of 1995 would be a period in which the energies of the people of Northern Ireland would be concentrated on the search for peace; instead, it was punctuated by a series of disputes concerning 'the rights to march'. These disputes seemed to come down to a simple question. What rights do organisations have to conduct a parade or demonstration in areas where a significant number of the population does not welcome them? This study aims to analyse the background to the parading disputes, examine the events of 1995, consider the attitudes of some of those directly involved in the disputes, and examine some of the proposals which have been made to resolve or improve the situation.

Parading is an established feature of life in Northern Ireland. According to the RUC *Chief Constable's Annual Report* in 1995, there were 3500 parades, the vast majority of which, 2574, were described as 'loyalist' and 285 were described as 'nationalist; 617 were categorised as 'other', and 24 as 'illegal'. Of the 3500, only 22 were re-routed or had other conditions placed upon them. Nevertheless, although the number of disputed parades is small the effect of those disputes upon community relations has been significant. The history of the north of Ireland over the last two hundred years is littered with incidents of civil disturbances connected to parades (see for instance Bardon 1992, and Wright 1987 & 1996). The inter-communal disturbances in 1969, that marked the start of the current version of what is known as 'the Troubles', were often sparked off by parades or demonstrations (Purdie 1990). Since then parades and demonstrations running each year from Easter right through to September, 'the marching season', annually raise tensions and require a massive amount of policing. In 1985 and 1986 parade disputes in Portadown, County Armagh, caused six major riots which not only added to the divisions between the Protestant and Catholic communities in the town but significantly soured the relationship between the RUC and the Protestant community. Since 1985 the number of parades in Northern Ireland has shown an increase of over 32% with loyalist parades increasing by 34% and republican parades by 16%. Further, whilst there are only a few incidents where significant confrontations take place, parades can be an annoyance to members of both the Catholic and Protestant communities and with the number of parades increasing the atmosphere in which the events take place may worsen.

We have divided this study into four major sections. Part one takes an overview of the parades. In particular we survey the history of the parades, and suggest why there are so many loyalist parades in comparison with nationalist and republican parades. The loyalist parading organisations are analysed, and from this we have created a typology and a chronology of parades. Local variations in parades and the importance of locality in the parading calendar are examined. We also trace the development of bands and band parades, focussing on their relationship with the Orange and other loyal Institutions. Finally, in the first part we look at the figures relating to the number of parades, attempting to explain why there has been a steady increase in overall numbers.

In Part Two we examine the parading disputes of 1995. Drawing predominantly from press reports, but also from interviews and our own presence on many of the occasions, we will discuss both the differences, and the links connecting, different disputes and the ways they were policed and mediated. Then we will explain who was in dispute and where most of the disputes took place.

Part Three concentrates upon the attitudes and perceptions that interested parties have, in respect to parade disputes, and examines the ways that opposed positions are understood and misunderstood. It then looks at the various suggestions made to try and resolve the disputes and improve the environment in which public political expression takes place. It sets out various issues: the role of mediators; some suggested guidelines for parades; the use and problems with laws governing parades; the ways in which organisers can be held responsible for parades; and the possibilities of introducing a parading commission or tribunal to arbitrate in disputes. We have not made recommendations, but have attempted to explicate a range of possibilities, and to analyse and explain the merits and problems of the various suggestions that have been made.

Finally, Part Four of the report looks briefly at the particular areas in which significant disputes took place in 1995 and summarises the overall findings.

We have drawn from a variety of sources: first, we have used the figures that are available on parades; second, we have made a detailed examination of press reports related to parades; third, we have tried to talk to as many of the interested and involved parties as possible in the limited time that was available to us - we hope that the views of all of those to whom we spoke are reflected at some point in the report, even if they have not been attributed by name; fourth, and finally, we have tried to draw upon our own experiences attending and watching parades over a number of years, as well as utilising some of the research that has been conducted into different public events around the world.

The authors of this study are under no illusions as to the difficulties in trying to solve particular disputes or improve the climate for political expression in general. The disputes over parades are a manifestation of the wider political divisions and any easing of the tensions over 'the right to march' relies to a great extent upon other political developments. Nevertheless, it is important that the area of public political expression is examined as part of the attempt to create a society within which diverse communities can be at ease.

PART 1

SECTION 1: PARADES - AN OVERVIEW

There is a long history of pseudo-military parades in the British Isles. In Ireland throughout the eighteenth century the government held annual parades to commemorate the Williamite revolution, but it was also common for formalised groupings such as the Freemasons, Journeyman associations and later the Volunteer Companies or irregular bands of citizens, Jacobite supporters and agrarian secret societies to parade themselves in public. Amongst the diverse group we now broadly define as the Protestant community, the right to bear arms in defence was in part seen as fundamental to their position as subject and citizen. Whilst in the rest of the British Isles there has been general agreement as to the nature of the state and the position of the subject within the state, the populous of Ireland has not shared in that security. As such, there have been social and political reason for the continued banding together of interested parties. The custom of holding parades is therefore not unique to Ireland but it has been extenuated by political circumstances. The political identity of the two dominant communities in the north of Ireland have thus become closely linked to the development of an extensive range of anniversaries marked by a parade (see 4.1).

The huge difference in the number and continuity of parades between the two communities can be partly understood in terms of their relationship to the state. Early Orange parades, at the end of the eighteenth century, were effectively encouraged by the state in order to oppose the rise of the United Irishmen. Until the 1870s the banding together of groups, Protestant and Catholic, resulted in frequent sectarian clashes and were consequently seen as a threat to the state. Parades were often an expression of sectarian, communal, opposition and were, at least officially, discouraged, re-routed or banned (Wright 1987, 1996). After 1870 the Orange Institution became more extensively patronised by both the landed classes and the Belfast bourgeoisie and it was used to mobilise opposition to the campaign for Home Rule and to create a distinctive British identity. The increased popularity and respectability allowed Orange parades to flourish whilst similar events which supported Home Rule, particularly in Ulster, were opposed. Even with the expansion of the nationalist Ancient Order of Hibernians at the start of the twentieth century the dominant position of Orange parades remained. Put simply, the number of places in which Orangemen were able to parade was always far higher than those open to nationalist parades. Any attempt by nationalists to parade in areas with anything less than a large Roman Catholic majority was quickly stopped.

This process reached fruition with the formation of Northern Ireland. Both the northern and southern states developed a collective identity which was based upon the single dominant ethno-religious group. Commemorative events which reflected this political identity were enshrined by the state while others were opposed. Orange parades in the south became increasingly difficult to organise as they came under threat from local IRA groups. In the north the Twelfth effectively became a ritual of state while nationalists were restricted to marching in a limited number of areas. In towns such as Lurgan, with a mixed population, nationalist parades often caused disturbances. Any Unionist politician who attempted to restrict an Orange parades came under enormous political pressure so that by the late 1950s there were even Orange parades taking place through the almost exclusively Roman Catholic town of Dungiven.

The relationship of the state to public expression in the form of parades has provided the environment for loyalist parades to flourish, whilst nationalist or republican parades have been restricted. This in itself goes a long way to explaining why loyalist parades are so numerous and apparently carry so much 'tradition'. They have so many 'traditional routes' simply because they have, certainly until the fall of Stormont, been in the political position continually to reassert those routes. The claim of 'tradition' is therefore closely linked to the historical power relations in Northern Ireland. But, as we will show, there is a strong decentralist and democratic tradition within the Protestant community. Many of the more parochial parades are important expressions of local identity, reasserting the social and political relationships within that community. This has perhaps been made more significant by the increased geographical dispersal of the population. The profligate number of small parades can therefore be understood in terms of the localised nature of the loyal orders and the social relationships they give expression to within their particular communities, as well as by examining the broader political environment.

In the following sections we will begin with an overview of the structure of the loyalist parading bodies. This will be followed by a typological description of their parades. We then consider the annual cycle of parades or the 'marching season' and discuss some of the local variations in parading practice. Finally Section Five offers an brief overview of the changes in parading culture over the past ten years.

SECTION 2: LOYALIST PARADING ORGANISATIONS

There are four main players involved in organising loyalist parades:
1. The Orange Institution (the Orange Order or 'the Orange').
2. The Royal Black Institution ('the Black').
3. The Apprentice Boys of Derry.
4. Marching bands.

As well as these, there are three less prominent bodies who organise regular parades:
5. The Independent Orange Institution.
6. The Junior Orange Institution (juveniles).
7. The Royal Arch Purple Institution.

Collectively these groups are responsible for approximately 2500 parades held each year. The three main bodies and the bands are responsible for the overwhelming majority of the parades. Parades organised by the Orange, the Black and the Apprentice Boys ('the loyal orders') are mutually exclusive, in that only one institution can be officially present at each parade. However, many individual are members of more than one of these organisations and therefore the separation of personnel in different parades is not so clear cut. The feature common to all the loyal orders is that membership is confined to Protestants.

2.1 The Orange Institution

In terms of both the size of the Institution and its political status, the Orange is the most important of the loyal orders. At its peak during the earlier part of this century it could probably boast 100,000 members, although in recent years membership has probably shrunk to nearer 40,000. There is scarcely a townland or village in Northern Ireland with a significant Protestant population that does not have an Orange lodge. Most villages have at least one Orange hall, and many have more than one.

The Orange Institution was formed in 1795 during sectarian clashes in County Armagh. To begin with it struggled to gain 'respectability', with the parades reflecting localised sectarian politics and frequently ending in civil disturbances. Those gentry that were involved in the Institution often failed to control the lower class membership. Only during the second half of the nineteenth century, as the threat of Home Rule grew, did substantial sections of the Protestant middle and upper classes become involved in Orangeism. With a few notable exceptions nearly all senior Unionist politicians since the 1870s have been members of the Institution. The Institution also has support from a significant number of the clergy in the larger Protestant churches and, until recently, was patronised by employers and large landowners. The Orange Institution has played a considerable role in the social, political and economic life of Northern Ireland.

The basic organisational structure was strongly influenced by Freemasonry (Dewar, Brown and Long 1967). Each member joins a local lodge at the invitation of members in that lodge. They are asked to meet the standards set by the 'Qualifications of an Orangeman'. These state that an Orangeman should have 'sincere love and veneration for his Heavenly Father ... a humble and steadfast faith in Jesus Christ ... believing him to be the only Mediator between God and man'. An Orangeman should 'cultivate truth and justice, brotherly kindliness and charity, devotion and piety, concord and unity, and obedience to the laws; his deportment should be gentle and compassionate kind and virtuous'. He should 'diligently study the Holy Scriptures ... love, uphold and defend the Protestant religion' and 'strenuously oppose the fatal errors and doctrines of the Church of Rome, and scrupulously avoid countenancing (by his presence or otherwise) any act or ceremony of Popish worship'. An Orangeman should 'by all lawful means, resist the ascendancy of that Church ... ever abstaining from all uncharitable words, actions, or sentiments, towards his Roman Catholic brethren'. His conduct should be guided 'by wisdom and prudence, and marked by honesty temperance and sobriety: the glory of God and the welfare of man, the honour of his Sovereign, and the good of his country, should be the motive of his actions' (Kennedy 1990, 1995).

To an extent then the Orange Institution can be seen as religious. However, in Northern Ireland joining the Institution is a political decision, as well as a religious one, and for most Orangemen parading in public is the focus of their membership. Indeed, many Orangemen would not regularly attend church or their Orange lodge meetings. Parades are therefore quite clearly political expressions and are understood in that way by the majority of participants. The Orange Institution is political.

There are about 1400 private lodges in Ireland, each with its own warrant number, its own particular history and to an extent its own character. Some lodges are based upon location, a particular village or district, or even upon an area where members used to live, such as lodges in Belfast that connect to the counties of Fermanagh, Tyrone or Donegal. Others are based upon occupations or even specific places of work, although such specific lodges are now less common. Some lodges are based upon a church, a bible class or perhaps a temperance or abstinence group, while others are named after and commemorate individuals, events or groups that have significant local historical bearing. There are also some, such as Eldon LOL No. 7 in Belfast, which are seen as elite lodges. Many members remain in their original lodges even though they now live some distance away, this can allow them to continue to identify with the area where they grew up. Each member is expected to pay annual dues and most lodges have regular monthly meetings which are often poorly attended. For many members their only involvement with a lodge is at the major parades.

Every lodge elects a number of officers annually. The most important are the Master, Deputy Master, Secretary, Treasurer and Chaplain. They are charged with looking after the social, financial and spiritual welfare of the lodge. This includes organising local parades and church services, the transport and catering at the Twelfth and other major events, and the hiring of a band. A lodge may well have a close relationship with a particular band although some lodges find it difficult to hire the sort of band they would like and therefore parade without one. The hiring of a band, the transport to parades, and especially the replacement of the lodge banner, can all impose great expense upon private lodges which generally have relatively little money.

Each private lodge sends six representatives to one of the 126 District Lodges in Ireland. The District Lodge also elects officers and is charged with the care of the private lodges within it, the upkeep of a District Orange Hall, and the organisation of parades at district level, particularly a mini-Twelfth. Most districts host the main Twelfth parade, and therefore entertain the surrounding Districts, on a regular cycle.

The District Lodge sends between 7 and 13 members to one of the 12 County Grand Lodges. As the next level of authority these can arbitrate on disputes and they help as general liaison in the organisation of the Twelfth parades within their area. Belfast, which has nine districts, has a single Twelfth parade which is organised by County officials. Districts also have their own character and often maintain a friendly rivalry as to which is the biggest, best, or smartest. There is, for example, a well known rivalry in Belfast between the two largest Districts, Sandy Row, District No. 5 and Ballymacarrett, District No. 6.

Finally the Grand Lodge of Ireland is made up of 250 representatives from the County Lodges and other elected Officers. According to a recent leaflet produced by the Grand Lodge, 86% of Districts are represented in some way in the Grand Lodge. All officers of the Grand Lodge are elected except for 2 Assistant Grand Masters, whose appointment is in the gift of the Grand Master, and 6 Deputy Grand Masters who are nominated by their County. Any major rule changes have to go through the Grand Lodge and they are the final arbiters of any disputes within the organisation, such as the disciplining of members. The Grand Lodge meets in full twice a year but also works through a number of committees, including the Education Committee, the Rules Revision Committee and the Press Committee. The Grand Lodge only organises parades occasionally, for anniversaries such as the Tercentenary of the Battle of the Boyne in 1990.

Historically, divisions between 'the rank and file membership' and the Grand Lodge are not uncommon and they can significantly influence Unionist politics in general. The Institution is a complex and disparate organisation with authority existing at numerous different levels and locations. To make sense of disputes over particular parades it is important to understand the role parades play in the internal politics of the Orange Institution. Central control over the other parts of the Institution is limited; County and District Lodges have a strong sense of local identity and will look to the Grand Lodge as the guardian of the Institution's image rather than for authority. This means that the Grand Master is often in the position of publicly defending the Institution over incidents and events over which, in truth, he has relatively little control. However, the nature of the hierarchy means that a Grand Master's position is a relatively safe one, his re-election often being rubber-stamped each year. Even in 1995 when there was clearly great dissatisfaction amongst a significant number of Orangemen with the role Martin Smyth played in the parading disputes, there was little chance of his not being re-elected.

It is important to recognise the relationship between the Orange Institution and the Ulster Unionist Party (UUP). The Orange Institution has a large representation on the Ulster Unionist Council, and many other delegates are also Orangemen. From 1921 to 1969 only three Cabinet members in Northern Ireland government's at Stormont were not at some point Orangemen. Of the Unionist MPs at Stormont that did not reach the Cabinet during that period, 87 out of 95 were in the Orange Institution (Harbinson 1973:90-91). The majority of the present Ulster Unionist MPs at Westminster are Orangemen. Whilst this relationship remained unproblematic for much of this century, the divisions within Unionism from the early 1960s onwards has made the relationship more complex. The significant overlap between senior members of the Orange Institution and the Ulster Unionist Party has meant that, at least at the top, the Institution has closely reflected the policies of the UUP. However, many Orangemen are supporters of Ian Paisley's Democratic Unionist Party (DUP). Paisley himself left the Orange Institution in 1962 after a number of disputes, and in particular over the restriction on Free Presbyterian Church ministers from becoming chaplains within the Institution (Moloney and Pollock 1986). Paisley is at present a member of the Apprentice Boys of Derry and he regularly speaks at the Twelfth organised by the Independent Orange Order. Nevertheless, he retains significant power within the Orange Institution. He is regularly invited to 'lodge' events such as the opening of arches and he has involved himself in some of the parading disputes that we will discuss. He effectively led the negotiations at Drumcree, he made the best received speech at the rally at Drumcree, and he was able to calm the crowd to some extent whilst negotiations proceeded. Whilst the Grand Master, Martin Smyth, left things to local Orange representatives and to the local MP David Trimble, Paisley was there in person. That situation said much about the Orange Institution and the dispersed authority structure within it.

The closeness of the relationship between the Orange Institution and political power, particularly during the Stormont era, is still significant both in terms of the feelings many nationalists have towards Orangeism and in terms of the large number of loyalist parades.

2.2 The Royal Black Institution
The relationship between the Royal Black Institution and the Orange Institution is so close that it is debatable whether one can see them as separate organisations. The Black can trace its routes almost as far back as the Orange. The early Orange Institution developed within it a series of 'degrees' through which members could proceed. Some of these, such as 'the Arch Purple', were officially sanctioned by the Grand Lodge. But others degrees were banned, since membership of them effectively offered routes to power which those in the Grand Lodge found difficult to control. Nevertheless, these alternative degrees continued to exist in some areas. One such degree was 'the Black'. In the 1850s, after some debate, the Royal Black Institution was officially constituted in its own right (McClelland 1968).

Individual members group together in Preceptories and the organisational structure in many ways mirrors that of the Orange Institution, to such an extent that some lodges and Preceptories contain largely the same personnel. Members of the Black are known as 'Sir Knights' and to be able to join one must already be a member of the Orange Institution. The Black is probably best differentiated from the Orange by being more religious and more 'respectable' but the Black, like the Orange, has also lost many of its professional and middle class members. The Black Institution is less overtly political and its banners and regalia reflect its religious bias, particularly through displays of Old Testament imagery (Buckley 1985-86; Buckley and Kenney, 1995). The institution is strongest in Counties Down and Armagh, but Black parades take place in all six counties of Northern Ireland although there is no major Black parade in Belfast. In general a Black parade has fewer 'blood and thunder' bands and more kilty (kilted bagpipe), silver and accordion bands. This is partly because the Institution has a more rural base and, as a rule, county parades are generally not as 'rough' as parades in Belfast. The Black Institution is therefore best understood as reflecting the more middle class, rural, religious, respectable, even elite, elements of Orangeism. It is the more conservative face of the Orange and of Unionism.

2.3 Apprentice Boys of Derry.

The Apprentice Boys are the smallest of the three loyal orders and have an estimated 12,000 members; however it is the most important such group in Londonderry. The organisation is independent from the other loyal orders, although many Boys are also members of the Orange Institution. In the past the Apprentice Boys have had institutional connections with the Ulster Unionist Party but now they are independent of all political parties. A number of leading unionist politicians, of both main parties, are members. The main purpose of the Apprentice Boys is to hold parades to commemorate the two principal events of the Siege of Derry: the closing of the city gates by the apprentice boys in December 1688, and the relief of the siege with the arrival of the Mountjoy in August 1689. These two events have been commemorated in the city in some form since the late 17th century.

The heart of the organisation are the eight Parent Clubs which are based in the Memorial Hall in Londonderry. Six of these are named after leaders of the siege: Baker, Browning, Campsie, Mitchelburne, Murray and Walker, the other two being the Apprentice Boys of Derry Club and the No Surrender Club. The first Apprentice Boys club was established in 1714 but the present organisation dates to 1814. The Baker Club was formed in 1927, the Campsie Club as recently as 1950, while the other five clubs were founded in the 19th century (Tercentenary Committee 1989). Membership of each of the eight Parent Clubs varies in size but their total membership is estimated at between 4-500 men. The Apprentice Boys do not have a junior organisation and have no female members.

Besides the Parent Clubs the organisation consists of around 200 Branch Clubs across Northern Ireland, in Scotland, England, the Republic and three in Canada. Each Branch Club is established through, and affiliated to, a Parent Club. Branch Clubs in each area are also linked together by Amalgamated Committees which function as sub-committees of the main organisation. There are eight Amalgamated Committees in Northern Ireland, one in Scotland and one in England. The Northern Irish Amalgamated Committees organise a parade on Easter Monday, the English and Scottish Amalgamated Committees also hold annual parades.

Overall organisation and management of the Apprentice Boys is controlled through the General Committee. This has 44 members in total and meets five times a year. Each of the eight Parent Clubs has four representatives on the General Committee, usually drawn from their officers. The remaining members of the General Committee are representatives of the Branch Clubs acting as officers of the Amalgamated Committee. All officers are elected annually, but retiring officers may be re-elected. The officer posts and their responsibilities are similar to those of the Orange Order. The General Committee also has a Chief Marshall and each Parent Club and each Branch Club is responsible for providing two marshals for parades. The overall structure means that the membership based in the city of Londonderry always has ultimate control over any decisions that are made, even though most Apprentice Boys live elsewhere.

2.4 The Bands
The common factor to all parades is the presence of marching bands. Historically most parades have had some sort of musical accompaniment. In the middle of the last century music was provided by informal 'drumming parties' involving large Lambeg-style drums and fifes. After the legalisation of parades in 1872 organised accordion, flute, and silver bands became prominent. Some bands, particularly in Belfast, were funded by factories and were of high quality, but drumming parties and rougher local bands always played a part in events, even if they were not approved of by senior Orangemen. From the end of the nineteenth century bands began to travel over from Scotland and these often had a reputation for being loud and enthusiastic. During the sectarian riots in Belfast in

1934, it was a Scottish band that was implicated in a number of incidents in the Docks area (Hepburn 1990). Accordion bands were for a long time the most popular style but since the war flute bands have grown in number.

Bands have always been a vital part of the parades and they play a central role in creating the mood of the event. This has been particularly obvious since the middle of the 1960s when what are known as 'blood and thunder' or 'kick the pope' bands have emerged (Bell 1990). These bands are often based in a particular street, district or village and their membership is predominately working class. Some bands have their own hall where they practice while others use Orange halls or other local facilities. Managing, and in particular financing, a band involves considerable organisation and most bands have a formalised organising committee with elected officers such as band captain, secretary and treasurer. Major decisions, on such matters as new uniforms, are taken by vote among the entire band.

The majority of bands have no formal allegiance to any of the loyal orders although individual members may often belong to one or more organisation, and in country areas there are still some bands that are formed out of Orange lodges. The majority of bands are independent, self-organising, bodies. At the same time a number indicate support for the loyalist paramilitary groups. This is often revealed through style of dress, and paramilitary symbols displayed on the uniforms, the bass drum and on flags. The loyal orders have made some efforts to control which sort of flags appear on their parades but the prominence given to the historical UVF in unionist sympathies means that UVF flags commonly appear at Orange parades. While the popularity of the Orange Institution, particularly amongst the young, and in Belfast, has declined, the popularity of bands has increased. The bands offer an alternative, less official, social network, and their involvement in parades is in many senses more 'active', and therefore more attractive, to younger and more alienated groups.

2.5 Other Parading Bodies
a. The Independent Orange Institution

The Independent Orange Institution was formed in 1903 as a breakaway from the Orange Institution. To begin with it was politically radical and drew support from the working classes in Belfast, who were demanding labour reforms, and tenant farmers in Antrim who were demanding land reforms. Although some of the early leaders held liberal views on the national question, many others were Protestant fundamentalists who campaigned strongly for keeping the Sabbath and restricting the consumption of alcohol. This fundamentalist element, largely based in north Antrim, came to dominate the organisation and by the 1920s the new institution's popularity had waned in Belfast (Boyle 1962-63, Morgan 1991, Patterson 1980).

The significance of the Independent Orange Institution was, and still remains, that it is not affiliated to any particular unionist party. This has meant that it can attract those who are disenchanted with the Ulster Unionist Party. In recent years, Ian Paisley, who is a member of neither institution, has always given a speech at the Independent Orange Twelfth. This allows him to remain distant form the Unionist Party yet still symbolically appear close to Orangeism. There has been a small growth of new Independent lodges in recent years, most significantly in Portadown in 1976 as a result of a disagreement with officers of the Grand Orange Lodge. Whilst they are not strong in numbers they do organise regular parades and they can be outspoken on the parading issue in general.

b. The Junior Orange Institution

Junior Orange Lodges appeared during the last century but it was not until 1925 that they came under the control of the Grand Orange Lodge of Ireland. In 1974 a Junior Grand Orange Lodge was formed and in recent years there has been an increase in interest in the organisation and a corresponding increase in the number parades organised. The Junior Institution takes boys up to the age of 16 when they pass into the senior lodge. Junior lodges are always closely connected to a senior lodge and, since many adults attend the junior events and both Junior and senior use the same bands, it is not always obvious when one is watching a parade of the Junior Institution.

c. The Royal Arch Purple

The Royal Arch Purple is even more closely tied to the Orange Institution than is the Black, but it is still technically a separate Institution. The first meeting of the Grand Royal Arch Purple Chapter of Ireland was in 1911. As with the Royal Black Institution it developed out of a series of Orange degrees and most Orangemen move rapidly into the Purple and Arch Purple degrees. The Purple has its own organisation which reflects its close association with the Orange Institution, it holds a number of church parades but does not have a major parading date (Murdie, Cargo, Kilpatrick nd).

SECTION 3: VARIETIES OF PARADES

This section offers a typology of parading based on the purpose of the parade rather than on the group organising the event. It is impossible to offer detailed numbers of the parades within each category as no statistical details are available, however an attempt is made to indicate the importance of each type of parade. Loyalist parades can be broken down into nine relatively discrete categories:

> 1. Main Commemorative Parades
> 2. Local Parades
> 3. Feeder Parades
> 4. Church Parades
> 5. Arch, Banner and Hall Parades
> 6. Social Parades
> 7. Occasional Parades
> 8. Competitive Band Parades
> 9. Commemorative Band Parades

3.1 Main Commemorative Parades
These are few in number but they are regarded as the most significant events of the marching season. Within this category are the Orange and Independent Orange Institution parades held each year on the Twelfth of July; the Black Demonstrations at Scarva on 13 July; in County Fermanagh in early August (which marks the battle of Newtownbutler); and the six Last Saturday parades at the end of August. Finally it includes the Apprentice Boys 'Relief of Derry' parade on or near 12 August.

These few dates form the heart of the parading calendar and constitute what most people understand as basis of the loyalist parading culture or tradition. They form only a small percentage of the total parades but they attract the largest numbers of both marchers and spectators. While all these parades have symbolic significance among the Ulster Protestants, it is possible to focus even more closely and say that the Twelfth of July and the Relief of Derry parades are the principal dates of the Marching Season.

The Boyne anniversary parades are always held on the twelfth of July itself and Scarva the day after, unless the day falls on a Sunday in which case they are held a day later. The Twelfth of July is a public holiday in Northern Ireland and has been since 1926. All the other parades are held on the nearest Saturday, although as recently as 1986 the Relief of Derry parade was held on the anniversary itself. The change to a Saturday was apparently made because many people found it difficult to attend on a week day.

Part of the significance of these events is their longevity as public celebrations. As anniversaries all are well established, and their continuing commemoration is integral to the sense of a Protestant identity. The Orange Order has held parades to commemorate the Twelfth of July since the year after its formation in 1795. However, the anniversary of the Battle of the Boyne was by then already a long established public event. The custom of holding a parade to remember the Boyne victory began in Dublin in the early 18th century and was taken up in Ulster by the 1770s.

Parades were often the cause of violent disturbances during the nineteenth century, and repeated attempts were made to impose legal restrictions in the early decades of the century, which were largely unsuccessful. However, between 1849 and 1872, the Party Processions Act was utilised to suppress most parades, including the Twelfth. Since the repeal of this legislation in 1872, and despite occasional violent outbursts, the Twelfth has never been banned. Parades have been held every year, except 1916 and during World War Two, when parades were voluntarily cancelled.

In the contemporary parading calendar the Twelfth is marked by 19 main parades across Northern Ireland, although the number of feeder parade boosts the total number of parades on the day. Statistics provided by the RUC Central Statistics Unit put the number of parades on the Twelfth in 1995 at 547. Eighteen of the main parades are organised by the Orange Institution and one by the Independent Orange Institution. Belfast and Ballymena each host a parade each year while the venues for the remainder are rotated. Some areas follow a regular cyclical pattern in which the Twelfth visits a town or village every 4, 7 or 11 years, while others follow a more irregular rotation. The decisions about the location of Twelfth parades is made at either district or county level of the Institution but the cycles appear to be largely ordered by tradition. The 17 venues outside Belfast are divided as follows:

County Antrim	6
County Armagh	1
County Down	4
County Fermanagh	1
County Londonderry	2
County Tyrone	3

The largest of these parades are those held in County Armagh, where Orangeism originated and has remained prominent, and in Belfast. Twelfth of July parades are largely local events at which the Orangemen parade through their home districts and counties, although substantial numbers of Orangemen and bands come over from Scotland for the day. After a morning parade, the men assemble at 'the field', where a religious service is held and, in many areas, leading Unionist politicians make speeches from the platform. In the afternoon a return parade completes the day's events.

In contrast, the main Apprentice Boys anniversary, the Relief of the Siege of Derry, is marked by a single parade in the city. This event attracts members and bands from across Northern Ireland and beyond. Apart from the parade, the main event is a service in St. Columb's Cathedral in the morning which is largely restricted to the members of the Parent Clubs. There is no public platform and there are no political speeches during the celebrations. The Relief of Derry has been commemorated with a parade of some sort since the early 18th century, while the anniversary has been organised by the Apprentice Boys clubs since they were reformed in the early 19th century. Until early this century the anniversary was still largely a local affair but the growth of the rail network made it possible for people to come from all over the north to attend the parade. Newspaper reports suggest that the Relief celebrations have been growing in popularity and in importance since the 1950s and the anniversary now attracts crowds comparable to the Belfast Twelfth.

The original route of the parade seems to have been largely restricted to a circuit of the city walls, but as the scale of the proceedings increased so too did the length of the route. Since the end of the Second World War the parade route has been regularly extended because of the numbers of people walking. One year it took in parts of the cityside area and the next year it would cross over onto the Waterside. Violent clashes at the event in 1969, and the subsequent arrival of British troops in the city, is widely accepted as marking the beginning of the Troubles although earlier attempts to hold civil rights parades in the city had already led to violence and raised tension. In 1970 the Relief parade was included within a blanket, six-month, Ulster-wide ban on parades. When the anniversary was commemorated the following year, the city walls had been closed and the parade was forced to accept a new route which took it away from the Cityside and kept it largely on the Waterside.

The Black parades are more recently established. The Sham fight at

Scarva, and parades to mark the battle of Newtownbutler in County Fermanagh, can be traced back to the 1830s, but they only became associated with the Royal Black Institution after the end of the First World War. Newspaper reports suggest that at this time that the Black began to grow in popularity and to organise more of its own parades.

The Black Institution is strongest in the eastern part of Ulster and in the rural areas. In general it has an older membership and parades are more gently paced, with a predominance of melody, pipe and accordion bands. However, the Belfast Black parades, with larger numbers of blood and thunder bands and a younger membership, has more of the atmosphere of the Orange Twelfth. The main Black event is held on the last Saturday (Black Saturday or Last Saturday) in August when six separate county parades are held across the North. Belfast Blackmen parade through the city in the morning but their main parade is held in either County Down or County Antrim. These last Saturday parades were only fully established in the inter-war years and they have traditionally marked the end of the Marching Season.

3.2 Local Parades

This category includes the Orange mini-Twelfth parades, which are held from mid-June through into early July, and an increasing number of Somme Commemorations which are held on, or near to, 1 July. It also includes the celebrations to mark the landing of King William at Carrickfergus in early June; the Black parades in Bangor in July and in Belfast in mid-August; and the Apprentice Boys 'Closing of the Gates' parade in December and the Apprentice Boys Amalgamated Committee parade at Easter. Although not all of these parades mark specific anniversaries, all of these events have become an important part of the wider commemorative cycle. They often function as a prelude to the main parades. They are more localised demonstrations of strength and support and they incorporate routes, areas and districts that are not included on the main parade routes into the larger cycle.

Some of these parades are well established: for example the anniversary of the Closing of the Gates in Derry, at the end of which the figure of Lundy is burnt, was celebrated in the 18th century. Many of the others are much more recent. Despite popular perceptions, the Somme parades, as annual events, only date back to 1950s, rather than to the immediate post-war years. However, in the early years of this century, it was quite common for small parades to be held in a wide diversity of locations on or around

1 July, which was the original anniversary date of the Boyne prior to 18th century calendrical changes. The parade held by the Apprentice Boys Amalgamated Clubs on Easter Monday and the Junior Orange parade on Easter Tuesday both date back to the 1930s. They do not mark any anniversary, but were originally held to counter the Republican parades held the day before, on Easter Sunday. The parade to mark William's landing at Carrickfergus has only been re-established in recent years.

The mini-Twelfth and Somme parades appears to be a category that is on the increase, although they still account for only a small proportion of the total number of parades. More mini-Twelfth parades seem to be held each year especially in the areas outside of Belfast, a factor which has increased the overall visibility of Orange parades in the build up to the Twelfth. For instance Portadown District introduced a mini-Twelfth parade in 1990, and each year this event is focused on a different theme of Ulster Protestant or Orange history (Jones et al., 1996:57). The mini-Twelfths are significant in so far as they bring all the district lodges together as a preparation for the Twelfth itself and this is also the only occasion, apart from the Twelfth, at which all the lodges' regalia and banners are displayed. As the mini-Twelfths may well be the only substantial Orange parade in many towns, and as they are usually held on a Saturday or on a weekday evening, these parades often attract substantial numbers of people onto the streets.

In Belfast, where the custom has become well established, the mini-Twelfth parades begin in early June with a parade in North Belfast. This is followed by parades from Clifton Street, the Shankill Road, Sandy Row, Ballymacarrett (both on 1 July) and finally in Ballynafeigh in early July. On these occasions the Orangemen and their bands walk a circuit which begins and ends at the local Orange Hall. Participation is largely, although not exclusively, restricted to lodges that are based at the hall. The mini-Twelfth parades from the Ballynafeigh and Shankill Road Orange halls have both been subjected to protests in recent years. The Blackmen from Sandy Row and Ballymacarrett organise similar local parades prior to the Last Saturday demonstrations in August.

3.3 Feeder Parades
These are small parades held on the day of the Main Commemorative parades. There would be numerous such parades on the Twelfth of July, in towns and villages across the north when lodges parade locally before taking a bus to the main venue or, in the case of the larger towns and

Belfast, parade from their local Orange Hall to the start of the main parade. A similar range of parades is held at the end of the day as lodges return to their halls. Feeder parades are therefore often (a) very small (b) held over very short, localised routes and (c) often held early in the morning, but they make up a substantial proportion of total numbers. Figures supplied by the RUC Central Statistics Unit put the total number of parades on the Twelfth in 1990 at 361, in 1992 at 428, and in 1995 at 547.

As a category, feeder parades can be divided into two distinct groups, those that lead directly to a main parade in the same location and those that are held prior to a parade held elsewhere. Examples of both types are held on the lower Ormeau Road. The parade from Ballynafeigh Orange Hall to the City Hall on the morning of the Twelfth is an example of the first type. In this case the Orangemen state that they are taking both the most direct route and the traditional route in order to join up with the main body of men. The Apprentice Boys parades at Easter and in August fall into the other type in which the Belfast Walker Branch Club parade from the Ballynafeigh Orange Hall along the Ormeau Road before boarding a bus to another town. The custom of parading to a bus before departing to a main venue seems to have its origin in an earlier era when lodges met at their local hall and then paraded together to a railway station to take the train to another destination. When buses and cars became a more popular mode of travel, the parade from the hall was retained although it now took a shorter route to meet the waiting transport.

The argument for tradition informs the logic of both of these parades from Ballynafeigh when they have been challenged. The Orangemen and the Apprentice Boys both argue that they have been walking the same route for many years and they will continue to do so to uphold their traditions. However, while the claim that the route along the Ormeau Road on the Twelfth is the most direct and obvious one to take is certainly true and strengthens their argument, it does not justify the argument of the Apprentice Boys. The use of a bus or cars to go to a parade elsewhere makes many of these feeder parades unnecessary except as a ritual display.

2.4 Church Parades

All of the loyal orders hold a number of church services on a range of Sunday afternoons throughout the marching season. On these dates a lodge assembles at the local Orange Hall before parading to the appropriate venue. Some parades and services involve only a single lodge while other dates are events which are recognised across the entire institution. The main services for the Orange Order are the Somme memorial service held in late June, the Boyne anniversary service on the Sunday prior to the Twelfth and the Reformation Day services in late October. The City of Belfast Black Chapter have a collective service on the Sunday preceding the Last Saturday demonstration. The main service for the Apprentice Boys is held in St. Columb's Cathedral as part of the August and December celebrations.

An individual lodge or a District may attend services in a number of different churches in the course of the year and therefore be involved in a number of distinct, but still traditional, routes. Although the church parades are numerous they are usually small and again they are predominately local affairs: the Boyne anniversary services, for example, are organised on a lodge basis. However, there are larger scale gatherings such as the Loyal Orange Widows Fund charity service which is held in the Ulster Hall in late April and is attended by members from all Belfast Orange districts.

In the main, church parades receive little attention: in part this is because they are held on Sunday afternoons, in part because they lack the colour of the other parades and in part because there are usually only one or two bands present and the music that is played is usually religious. Church parades have little of the appeal of the larger commemorative parades and attract few spectators. However they can still have a symbolic significance as the events after the Drumcree church service last summer illustrate only too well.

3.5 Arch, Banner and Hall Parades

These are held on the occasion of the opening of an Orange Arch, an Orange Hall or at the unfurling of a new banner. There are always a number of such parades organised by Orange lodges in late June and early July and by Black Preceptories in August. They seem to be most common in smaller towns and rural areas. Some arch-opening ceremonies have been incorporated into mini-Twelfth parades, if they are not, they afford the occasion for a small parade. Banner unfurlings are occasional events which are held to mark the purchase of a new lodge banner. A banner can last upwards of 25 years if it is properly cared for, and so these are rare events for an individual lodge, they may be held perhaps only once in a generation. All of these are small local events, and there will rarely be more than one or two lodges present, although at least one band will be used to accompany the new banner as it is paraded through the area for the first time. Senior political figures are usually invited to these occasions, to help in the ceremonies, and to say a few words to the assembled constituents: but often they are also used as a platform for rallying the party faithful. As such they contribute both to the general build up to the Twelfth and reaffirm the political allegiances of Orangeism.

3.6 Social Parades
This is little more than a catch-all category to accommodate the few remaining parades held by the loyal orders. Within this group can be included the (increasing) range of parades held by the Junior Orange Order and the occasional parade organised by the Women's Orange Institution. The Belfast area juniors hold a parade on Easter Tuesday and a number of other districts hold parades at other times of the year. On each occasion a short parade is held from the Orange Hall to a waiting bus and then the district usually goes to a coastal town, where, after another short parade, the boys have a day by the sea. Although organised under the auspices of the Junior Orange Institution there are usually as many adults as juniors on the parade, accompanying the boys and playing in the bands.

3.7 Occasional Parades
There are also occasions when parades are held as a one-off event, sometimes as a special commemoration, and sometimes as part of the broader political process. For example, in 1990 the Orange Order held a special parade in Belfast to mark the Tercentenary of the Battle of the Boyne. In November 1994, shortly after the two paramilitary ceasefires had been called, the Orange Order paraded to a convention in the Botanic Gardens in Belfast. Here prominent members spoke on the theme of 'British Citizens demand British Rights'. In 1995, Orangemen held parades to mark the 50th anniversary of VE Day in May, and throughout the year a number of events were held to mark the Bicentenary of the Order itself, culminating in a series of parades and a rally in Loughgall, County Armagh, in September.

3.8 Competitive Band Parades
As well as taking part in all the above categories of parades the bands participate in an extensive range of parades which are organised by other bands. Band parades have become extremely numerous in recent years. They are held on most if not all Friday evenings, Saturday afternoons and Saturday evenings from the beginning of the marching season at Easter

until the end of September. Many of the well-established bands have a regular date for their parade, and new bands may find it difficult to find a suitable date in the main part of the marching season. This has let to an extension of the marching season and on many weekends band parades are held at a number of locations. The parades are primarily social events although there is also a competitive side to them. A range of trophies are offered by the host band who judge the visiting bands on a number of different categories such as their appearance, their deportment and their musical abilities as they parade around the host town.

The success of a parade depends heavily on reciprocity. If a band wants to attract a large number of visiting bands to its own parade it must in turn travel to a good number of other parades. The largest band parades can easily attract 50 or more bands, and these are therefore second only to the Main Commemorative parades in their scale and in the numbers of people who turn out to walk. These parades often dominate a small town from early evening until midnight and draw substantial numbers of young spectators into town and onto the streets; they therefore also generate a good trade for publicans, shopkeepers and diverse food stalls.

Many of the bands do not take the competitive element very seriously but the parades have become a prominent part of their social life. Some bands will parade at three or more such events in a weekend, week in week out throughout the season. Some bands may only need to go a few miles to attend a parade but others are prepared to hire a bus and travel across the province regularly. These band parades build up and consolidate an extensive network of social relations which is connected to, but distinct from, the more established networks of the loyal orders.

3.9 Commemorative Band Parades

These appear to be similar to the competitive band parades in so far as they are largely made up of the marching bands, but they are held as anniversary commemorations. There are two types of commemorative parades. One would include the parades held to mark the battle of the Somme in July or Armistice Day in November. On these occasions the bands and representatives of the loyalist paramilitary groups lay wreaths at local commemorative plaques or murals. Such events may be held at the same time as official events that are taking place elsewhere.

Another type of commemorative parade has begun to be held to mark the anniversary of the death of loyalist paramilitary figures who have died in the Troubles. Although small in number they can attract substantial numbers of bands and spectators. Once again wreaths are laid against murals or against commemorative plaques. Members of the Orange Institution and representatives of the paramilitary groups may both take part in these ceremonies.

SECTION 4: AN AVERAGE PARADING YEAR

The widely expressed importance given to the concept of tradition, and the emphasis placed on traditional parades, would suggest that a fairly consistent formal or regular pattern would underpin the parading year or marching season. But what exactly constitutes an average marching season? While there is a consistency at the heart of the loyalist parading calendar, it is difficult to be precise about what would constitute an average year. Most people would base such a year around the large traditional parades held on the Twelfth of July or the celebrations to mark the Relief of Derry, but these anniversaries constitute only a small proportion of the parading year. Furthermore, there can be a great deal of variation in the number of parades from year to year and from place to place.

There are number of ways that this issue can be approached. One way would be to consider an overview of the year through the calendrical cycle and describe all the anniversaries and commemorations that are marked by parades. Such a process would have to balance the general details that are applicable to all areas of Northern Ireland as well as note the regional variations. No two towns or villages, counties or districts, or even areas of towns or cities are the same as regards the overall parading calendar. Each town has its own traditions and its own customs and local parades which are organised in parallel with the more widely known major events. The local parading calendar may also vary from year to year depending on whether a town is to host a major parade, such as the Twelfth, or the Last Saturday of August parades. Some places will always have significantly larger numbers of parades than others. The total number of parades is boosted by a large number of small social parades which only continue, and may increase in number, in response to the enthusiasm of the participants and organisers, rather than through the dictates of tradition.

A second way would be to consider the marching season from the position of the various participants: a single individual, an Orange Lodge, a Black Preceptory and a marching band will all have a different perception of what constitutes an average year. The first part of this section describes the main events on the parading calendar as a chronology of an average year. The second part considers some of the variation in different towns and villages, while the third part considers the marching season from the perspective of a number of marching bands. Another approach, which will be considered in Section 5, would be to focus on the total number of parades and consider how the parading calendar and the number of parades varies. This might help to identify changing patterns and raise questions as to why the patterns are in fact changing. This in turn will raise questions about the issue of tradition: how long does a parade have to be held before it becomes 'traditional'? How regularly does a parade have to be held for it to remain 'traditional'? How much variation can be imposed on a parade route before it loses it 'traditional' character?

4.1 Chronology of the Main Parades

This chronology focuses on the parades organised by the loyal orders. Running parallel with these events is the band-parading calendar which begins in April and includes at least one parade most Friday evenings, Saturday afternoons and Saturday evenings until the end of September.

> *EASTER* - Some Orange lodges hold church parades on the Sunday nearest to St. Patrick's Day, 17 March, and Larne Juniors parade to church on Palm Sunday. But for most the Marching Season begins on Easter Monday when the Amalgamated Committee of the Apprentice Boys hold their parade. The organisation rotates among the several local committees and therefore the venue changes each year. Members from all parts of the Province assemble for this parade. The following day, Easter Tuesday, the Belfast and South Antrim lodges of the Junior Orange Order have their annual parade, usually at a coastal town. The final large gathering is held on a Sunday afternoon at the end of April when the Belfast Orange Lodges attend a charity service in the Ulster Hall, in aid of the Belfast Loyal Orange Widows Fund.

> *MAY* - This is a quiet month. There are no major parades, although a number of church parades are held, including annual services in County Cavan and County Monaghan. The Scottish Apprentice Boys hold their annual parade around the middle of the month. At the end of the month the Junior Orangemen from Armagh, South Tyrone and Fermanagh hold their annual parade - again at a coastal town.

> *JUNE* - In June the Marching Season begins to get fully under way. The first Orange mini-Twelfth parade is held on the first Friday in June in north Belfast, and the Belfast Branch Clubs of the Apprentice Boys parade on the first Saturday. On the second Saturday King William's landing is commemorated in Carrickfergus, and Portadown District Orangemen hold their mini-Twelfth parade. Mini-Twelfths are held in

north Belfast on the following weekend and a week later in west Belfast and in the Sixmilewater District of south Antrim.

JULY - The first of July, the anniversary of the beginning of the battle of the Somme, is second only to the Twelfth in the Orange calendar. Church parades are held on the nearest Sunday and, on the first itself, parades and wreath-laying ceremonies are held across the north. In 1995 long established parades were held in south and east Belfast, and others were reported in Armagh, Ballyronan, Castlederg, Cloughmills, Dromore, Dunmurry, Killylea, Lisburn, Lurgan, Markethill, Omagh, Poyntzpass, Rathfriland and Stewartstown on either 30 June or 1 July.

On the first Wednesday after the Somme parades, Belfast's Ballynafeigh District hold their mini-Twelfth parade; and, on the Saturday before the Twelfth itself, Orange parades are held in Rossnowlagh, County Donegal, and at a number of venues in Scotland. The following day, the Sunday before the Twelfth, or on the Twelfth itself, if it falls on a Sunday, the Boyne anniversary church service is held at venues across the north.

The Twelfth of July is the highlight of the Marching Season for most people. The nineteen parades are held at locations across Northern Ireland. Apart from Belfast and Ballymena, a different range of venues is used each year. Twelfth parades have been held at over 130 different locations since 1968. The Twelfth is the climax to the series of small parades that have been taking place for the previous few weeks and it also marks the end of the Marching Season for the Orange Institution (with the exception of the Reformation Day church services in October).

The following day the first major Royal Black Institution parades are held at Scarva and Bangor in County Down. Scarva is the traditional venue for the main parade of the County Down and County Armagh Preceptories. It is also the occasion for the Sham Fight, which is held near a tree under which King William reputedly rested on his way south. The Lurgan District Blackmen go to the seaside for the day.

AUGUST - The Twelfth traditionally marked the beginning of the two-week holiday period and no major parades are during this time, although band parades may take place at the weekends. There is a gap of almost a month before the next important parade, which is broken only by minor parades. The East Belfast Junior Orange lodges have an annual outing to the seaside at the beginning of August and some District Black Preceptories have their annual church parades at this time.

Parading restarts in earnest on the Saturday nearest 12 August. On this day the Apprentice Boys parade through the city to celebrate the Relief of Derry, and the County Fermanagh Blackmen parade, at a rotating venue, to mark the battle of Newtownbutler. The Fermanagh parade attracts members from across the border, but the Londonderry parade draws people from all areas of Northern Ireland and beyond. The parade is second only to the Boyne anniversary as the major event of the season.

The second half of August is dominated by Black parades. Local parades are held in south and east Belfast as a prelude to the main County Black parades on the Last Saturday. On this day parades are held in Counties Antrim, Down and Londonderry and in both east and west Tyrone. The Belfast County Preceptories alternate their parade between a venue in County Down and one in County Antrim.

SEPTEMBER AND OCTOBER - The Last Saturday formally marks the end of the commemorative marching season, but the band parades continue through September although by the end of the month the evenings are too short, and often too cold, to make parading attractive either for large numbers of bands or spectators. The last official Orange Institution parade of the year is held on the last Sunday in October on the occasion of the Reformation Day services. In Belfast all Orange Districts independently parade to St. Anne's Cathedral for the service.

NOVEMBER - A number of loyalist bands hold short parades to local memorials on Armistice Day, 11 November.

DECEMBER - The final parade of the year is held on the Saturday nearest 18 December in Londonderry, to mark the anniversary of the Closing of the Gates in 1688, the event that led to the Siege of Derry. This parade is much smaller than the August parade in the city and is largely of local interest. The climax of the day is the burning of the eighteen-foot high effigy of Lundy in the late afternoon.

This chronology shows that the three prominent parading bodies, the Orange, the Black and the Apprentice Boys have different and distinct parading calendars. The parades organised by the Orange Institution are largely held in the period of June to mid-July, although there are church parades both before and after these dates. From 13 July through to the end of August, the parades are organised by the Royal Black Institution, an organisation with a strong rural base and a more respectable and less popular character to it. In contrast the three main Apprentice Boys parades are almost equally spaced across the year: they begin the loyalist Marching Season at Easter, provide a second, popular climax in August and bring the cycle to an end in December. Although the main anniversaries, the Twelfth of July and the Twelth of August, Scarva and the Last Saturday are focused on one or more main parades, each day is also the occasion for numerous small parades by Orangemen, Blackmen and Apprentice Boys as they parade in their home localities before moving on to the main event. It becomes almost impossible therefore to document the marching season in its entirety or in its full complexity. This will be clear when we consider the overall scale of the parading calendar and the increase in parades over recent years.

4.2 Local Variations

The above chronology has been biased towards parades held in Belfast, but there does appear to be more parades, held on more dates, in the city than in other locations. In part this reflects the strength of the loyal orders among the Belfast working class, but it is also in part due to the desire not to have an overlap of parades in different areas of the city. The Belfast marching season is therefore the most extensive in so far as it is spread over more weeks than in other areas: mini-Twelfth parades are held regularly from early June to mid-July and when band parades and Black parades are included, there is probably a loyalist parade of some kind in Belfast on most, if not every, weekend during June, July and August.

This extensive sequence includes both 'Orange' and band parades. The 'Orange' parades are in turn based on the numerous Orange halls throughout the city. The decentralised structure of the loyal orders means that nobody is necessarily aware of the scale of the broader picture across the city. The same is true of the smaller towns and villages where once again the emphasis is on very localised traditions and practices. Even confirming the details of the range of parades from a single hall can prove difficult. The number may vary according to the number of Orange lodges and Black Preceptories based at a hall, and whether there are also Junior lodges, women's lodges, Purple Chapters and Apprentice Boys clubs or even affiliated bands who parade from a particular hall.

The Ballynafeigh district parades have proved the most contentious in recent years and there has been considerable uncertainty as to the total number of parades, and this has added to the suspicions and mistrust on both sides. Claims of 17 or more parades along the Ormeau Road each year, put forward by members of the Lower Ormeau Concerned Community (LOCC), have been strongly denied by the Orangemen. The fact that parades from Ballynafeigh were opposed on eight occasions only seems to contradict the LOCC claim. However, those parading argue that a single parade includes both outward and return legs, while the residents' group define this as two separate parades through their area, since they occur at two distinct times of day. So what are eight parades for the loyal orders would be seen as up to sixteen parades to the residents. Changes to the return route of some of the parades in recent years has also helped to confuse the issue.

The information we have suggests that eleven annual parades leave Ballynafeigh Orange Hall, although special anniversary parades may increase this number. There is also an annual band parade unconnected to the 'Orange' parades. Eight of these parades seek to walk the length of the Ormeau Road. These include four Orange, two Black and two Apprentice Boys parades. Two others, the mini-Twelfth and a junior Orange parade, have, in the past, followed a similar route but they have now been rerouted. The Boyne Anniversary church parade remains in the Ballynafeigh area. In recent years the return routes of the main parades have been diverted away from the lower Ormeau area, so that last year the loyal orders had intended to walk the length of the road twelve times on eight different days, beginning on Easter Monday and ending at the end of October.

This would seem to be the average number of parades that one might expect to find leaving each of the five main Orange halls in Belfast, although the smaller halls would probably have less. Outside Belfast a similar variety exists between those small halls at which only one or two lodges are based and the larger district halls. In Saintfield the district Orange lodge holds a Boyne church parade and a mini-Twelfth annually, and hosts the Twelfth in rotation with a number of other districts. Individual lodges may parade only three or four times a year. Residents report a similar small number of parades through the nationalist village of Bellaghy: the local loyal orders hold two annual church parades, and they also parade the main street before departing for both the Twelfth and Last Saturday parades - which are only occasionally held in the village. These small parades appear to cause little friction but there is strong opposition to the larger mini-Twelfth band parade in early July.

In Larne there are eleven parades from the Victoria Orange Hall between late March and the end of October. These are the responsibility of a wide range of bodies: four parades are organised by the Orange Order and two each by the Black, the Apprentice Boys and Junior Orange Order while the local Royal Arch Purple Chapter has a single church parade. As in all areas there will also be a range of one-off parades for the unfurling of banners, lodge anniversaries and for women's church services. A similar pattern emerges from Portadown where there are at least twelve parades each year from the Carleton Street Hall. These include five Orange parades, including three church parades, three Black, three Apprentice Boys and one Junior Orange parade. As in Belfast there will be other parades leaving each of the town's Orange Halls and as well as this there are three annual band parades in the town.

Over the marching season it is not unusual for a town to host a parade every 2-3 weeks on average, although these will be the responsibility of several different organising bodies and few individuals will necessarily have a view of the overall picture. Despite these large numbers of different parades, most individual members of the loyal orders are unlikely to parade more than half a dozen times each year and many will wear their sash even less. However, more senior figures and officers at the district level and above, may be expected to turn out on many more occasions, especially those who belong to two or more of the orders. Most members of the loyal orders will only parade in the area where they live, or the area in which they grew up, and, apart from those men who travel some distance to the Apprentice Boys parades, they will only rarely be involved in parades outside their home county.

4.3 Band Parading Practices
Although the loyal orders are most clearly identified with the tradition of parading, members of the numerous bands attend more parades than do members of the loyal orders. While bandsmen often do not have any formal connection with any of the loyal orders, they will parade at Orange, Black and Apprentice Boys parades. Many bands have established a regular contract with a particular lodge, preceptory or club and will lead them on parade year in and year out. This relationship may be with a lodge close to the band's own base, but some bands regularly parade away from their home areas at the big parades. This diverse range of connections with each of the different orders means that the bands parade in a much wider range of locations than do members of the loyal orders, and that they

parade at a greater number of parades overall. Where an Orangeman may only walk on the mini-Twelfth, the Twelfth and one or two church parades in his own area, a bandsman may cover a dozen or more parades at a bare minimum, and he may travel the length and breadth of Northern Ireland in the process, and include occasional trips to Scotland as well.

Although the bands seem to be a support act at parades organised by the loyal orders, for many of the spectators it is the bands that provide both the entertainment and the spectacle at these events. As one person told us - No-one is going to stand on the street to watch a few hundred Orangemen walk by, unless there are a few bands and some music as well'. Members of the loyal orders and newspaper reports also regularly judge the scale of a parade by the number of bands present, rather than by the number of members of the organising body.

The marching bands themselves can be grouped into a number of discrete categories. The most popular form is the flute band, which comprise a bass drum, four or more side drums and anything from a dozen to thirty-plus flautists. The marching flute bands can in turn be subdivided into 'blood and thunder' and 'melody' styles. The former play a single keyed flute, the latter use a five keyed instrument, even though it can be difficult to discern the difference on the parades. Flute bands are predominately male, but girls often form the colour party. In contrast, women and girls often play a prominent role in the accordion bands, who play a less raucous music based on accordions, side drums and a bass drum. Pipe bands, silver bands and full music flute bands also take part in some parades, particularly Black parades and those in rural areas. Many of the blood and thunder and melody bands parade regularly in competitions throughout the marching season, but the most important events remain the commemorative parades. The quality of a band is determined not so much by the number of trophies they win in competition but by the ease with which they get booked to attend the big parades.

While the bands display a considerable range in the total number of parades they attend, even a band that parades only at 'Orange' events is out more often than the vast majority of Orangemen. The blood and thunder bands concentrate on the main commemorative events and few of them play at church parades, where accordion or silver bands are more widely used. There is also less demand for blood and thunder bands in the rural areas, where traditional bands are preferred and lambegs are still often used to accompany a lodge. This can be illustrated by a comparison of the two Black parades held on 13 July 1994. The Lurgan town preceptories

Parade and Protest

who paraded in Bangor were accompanied by 10 blood and thunder bands, 2 accordion bands and a single traditional flute band; in contrast, at the county parade in rural Scarva there were 20 accordion bands, 19 flute bands, 18 pipe bands and 12 blood and thunder bands.

Table 4.1: Events attended by a sample range of bands.

This table shows a sample of the range of parades attended by different bands, which are labeled A to H. All are blood and thunder except B which is a melody flute band. All competed in numerous band parades last year except A which was restructuring and training new members. A and B are based in north Belfast, C and D are from south Belfast area, E is from Co. Down, F from Co. Tyrone and G and H are from Co. Armagh.

PARADE	A	B	C	D	E	F	G	H
AB Easter	Y	Y	Y	Y			Y	Y
Juniors		2	Y				Y	Y
Mini-Twelfths	4	3	4	2	1	2	3	2
Church							5	
Twelfth	Y	Y	Y	Y	Y	Y	Y	Y
Scarva							Y	Y
Relief of Derry	Y	Y	Y	Y			Y	Y
Last Saturday	Y	Y	Y	Y	Y	Y	Y	Y
Loughgall	Y	Y	Y				Y	Y
Loyalist Ceasefire	Y	Y	Y		Y		Y	Y
Armistice Day		Y	Y			Y		
AB December	Y		Y	Y		Y	Y	Y
Band Competitions	1	16	c40	c20	c25	c25	40+	c30
Other	2	2	2			2	2	
Total	14	30	c52	25+	c30	35+	c60	40+

Blood and thunder bands also dominated the recent Apprentice Boys Closing of the Gates parade in December 1995, which included only one accordion band and two traditional flute bands among the 22 which paraded the city. Only five of these bands were based in Derry. Although other bands had come from nearby villages like Burntollet and Newbuildings, six bands had travelled from the Belfast area and others were from Antrim, Castlederg, Garvagh, Markethill and Millisle.

When travelling to 'Orange' parades the bands may have their costs covered by the lodge they accompany, but they also travel extensively to band parades and it is the ever increasing number of these that provides the main social occasion for the bandsmen. It is at these events that networks of friendship and rivalry between bands are built and sustained. But they must be worked on to be maintained and so bands must constantly attend other parades. A few examples to illustrate this point: the Red Hand Defenders parade in Downpatrick, held at the end of the marching season in September, drew 19 bands. Many of these were from nearby: Crossgar, Killyleagh and Inch. But others came from further afield: Banbridge, Belfast, Bessbrook, Kilkeel, Lisburn, Newtownards, Rathfriland and Waringstown. Some of the big band parades in Belfast attract 40 or more bands from as far as Ballymena, Castlederg, Coleraine, Londonderry, Markethill, Portadown and smaller places in between. The biggest parades in recent years in Ballymena and Markethill, draw bands from a similar broad area. One Belfast band travelled to Antrim, Ballymena, Ballymoney, Clogh Mills, Craigavon, Crossgar, Donaghadee and Maghera last year, as well as playing at numerous parades in the Greater Belfast area, while one of the Portadown bands played at competitions in Belfast, Enniskillen and Londonderry and numerous places nearer to home.

The growth in numbers of blood and thunder bands, and the parallel development of band parades, marks a 'new wave' in the loyalist parading culture. At the same time the heightened visibility of bandsmen in often elaborate uniforms, along with the adoption of paramilitary insignia and symbols on band regalia, have made the bands an easy target to be represented as the 'cause' of problems and violence at parades. However, as we indicate later, band parades themselves only rarely provoke protests or degenerate into violence. Band parades are less easily cloaked in the garments of tradition and are therefore more easily restricted under public order legislation. Most band parades are kept away from nationalist areas and only in isolated cases have bands demanded the right to march into the centre of marginal or mixed areas. This is not to suggest that individual bands or bandsmen do not increase tension or animosity by playing party tunes or playing louder at particular places, but that this largely happens at parades organised by the loyal orders.

SECTION 5: OVERVIEW OF PARADES 1985-95

The only statistics on parade numbers are those published in the RUC *Chief Constable's Annual Report* each spring. These give bare figures on the total numbers of parades held by each community in the previous year, and the number of parades that had conditions imposed on them or at which trouble occurred. They can also be used to illustrate changes that have occurred over recent years. Prior to 1985 no figures for the numbers of parades were published in the report.

As this report was going to press we were given access to some more detailed statistics by The RUC Central Statistics Unit. They should allow us to analyse some trends in a future publication. However, the figures for 1995 appear to show a continuation of the trend over the past ten years in which the number of parades, both loyalist and republican have increased. In 1995 there were 3500 parades, of which 2581 were 'loyalist', 302 were categorised as 'nationalist', and 617 were placed in a new category of 'other'. Of these, seven loyalist parades and seventeen nationalist parades were illegal, thirteen loyalist and seven nationalist parades were re-routed, and two nationalist parades had other conditions placed upon them. The RUC calculate that disorder occurred at thirteen parades, eleven 'loyalist' and two 'nationalist'.

5.1 Ten Year Overview

Table 5.1 lists the numbers of parades that have been recorded in Northern Ireland from 1985 until 1994. These figures show that the re-routing of parades has been a consistent problem for the RUC. At the same time, those parades that have been re-routed account for only a small percentage of the total number of parades. In 1994 there were more parades re-routed than in any other year, and yet they still accounted for only just over 1% of all parades. The relatively high numbers of re-routed parades in 1985 are linked to the disputes at Portadown which have been analysed in Bryan, Fraser and Dunn (1995).

The figures also show two distinctive features that require explanation: first the increase in the number of parades over the ten year period, and second the large difference between the numbers of Loyalist and Republican parades. We have already suggested some of the reasons why parading is so prominent within the Ulster loyalist community: the historical background to loyalist parades, the connections to the Stormont state, and the importance of local parades in reasserting the idea of Northern Ireland

Table 5.1 Total number of parades in Northern Ireland between 1985-94.

	Total	Loyalist	Republican	Re-routed	Disorder/Conditions Imposed
1994	2792	2520	272	29	-
1993	2662	2411	251	12	-
1992	2744	2498	246	16	-
1991	2379	2183 (2)	196 (2)	14	1
1990	2713	2467 (1)	246	10	1
1989	2317	2099 (1)	218 (1)	14	5
1988	2055	1865 (4)	190 (4)	10	21
1987	2112	1863 (49)	249 (47)	11	18
1986	1950	1731	219	9	-
1985	2120	1897	223	22	-

Source: RUC Chief Constable's Annual Report and RUC Information Department.

i. The terms 'loyalist' and 'republican' are those used by the RUC, although in 1994 they changed the second of these categories to 'nationalist'. There is at present no way to sub-divide these gross numbers in terms of the bodies organising the parades.

ii. The figures in brackets refer to illegal parades, i.e. those parades that refused to seek formal permission from the RUC under the terms of the 1987 Public Order (NI) Order. Under this legislation organisers of parades were required to give seven days notice of the intention of holding a parade and give information regarding participants and the route to be taken. In the first year of the legislation a relatively high number of parades were deemed to be illegal. Between 1992 and 1994 there were no illegal parades.

as a Protestant state. These matters all require more detailed analysis than can be presented in this report, although consideration of the broader social, political and historical background is available elsewhere (Bryan 1994, Bryan and Officer 1995, Bryan and Tonkin in press, Jarman 1992, 1993, 1995, in press). Here we will concentrate the general increase in parades in recent years.

5.2 Growth in Parade Numbers

The average number of parades each year has increased substantially in the past ten years, from a low of 1950 in 1986 to a high of 2792 in 1994. This is a gross increase of over 43%. However this growth has been neither consistent nor steady but instead seems to have developed in two stages, giving three distinct average periods. In the first four years, from 1985 to 1988, the gross figure varied between 1950 in 1986 and 2120 in 1985 with an annual average of 2059. In both 1989 and 1991 the figures rose to over 2300 while in 1990 there was an even larger number of parades (2713). However, this figure was boosted because 1990 was the Tercentenary of the Battle of the Boyne and the Orange Institution held a series of extra events over the year. The average numbers of parades for the last three years, 1992-4, has now reached 2732, which is greater than in the Tercentenary year.

Table 5.2 presents the gross figures as averages in each of the three blocks of years.

Years	Average Total	Average Loyalist	% Total	Average Republican	% Total
1992-94	2732	2476	90.6	256	9.4
1989-91	2469	2249	91.1	220	8.9
1985-88	2059	1839	89.3	220	10.7

This table shows that the average number of loyalist parades has increased steadily over the three periods. In contrast, the average number of Republican parades was steady between 1985-91 and has only increased in the final period, between 1992-94. Furthermore not only have Loyalist parades increased in real terms they have also increased in percentage terms. Loyalists now organise a larger proportion of the parades than they did in the late eighties, and they now account for 90.6% of the total number of parades. Over the total period of 1985-94 the annual average number of parades increased by 32.7%; however, the annual average number of Loyalist parades increased by 34.6% whereas the annual average number of Republican parades increased by only 16%.

Accounting for this increase is another problem. The jump in figures in 1989 and 1990 is probably largely due to the Tercentenary anniversaries of the Relief of Derry and the Battle of the Boyne respectively. On both occasions extra effort was put into marking the anniversaries. The *Chief Constable's Annual Report* acknowledges the significance of the Tercentenary but suggests that the increase in 1989 was due to elections that took place that year. If the increase was purely for such specific one-off reasons it would be expected that parade numbers would drop in subsequent years, which has not happened.

The reason for the continued increase since 1992 is not so apparent. There is an increase of over 45% in loyalist parades between the number held in 1986 and the number held in 1994, a period when an extra 789 parades were recorded. The question would be more easily addressed if a greater range of information was available from the RUC, particularly giving figures by organisation. However, some figures supplied by the RUC Central Statistics Unit, shown in figure 5.3, seems to suggest that the numbers of parades on the Twelfth alone are rising.

Table 5.3 presents Number of Parades held on the Twelfth from 1990 to 1995.

Year	Number
1990	361
1991	386
1992	428
1993	389
1994	463
1995	547

(Statistics provided by the RUC Central Statistics Unit).

The annual changes in these figures could be accounted for by the changes in venues that take place discussed in section 3.1. Nevertheless, in terms of the wider debate over the issue of parading, all the above figures taken together are significant, particularly with regard to the importance of the concept of tradition, which is so often invoked by loyalist groups. On these statistics alone the idea of an unchanging and consistent tradition is seriously challenged. However, some scepticism has been expressed over the scale of loyalist parades with suggestions that the increase may be due to changes in the ways in which parades are counted or statistics processed rather than reflecting a real increase.

It would, therefore, seem reasonable to speculate that a large proportion of the general increase would be taken up by two specific categories of loyalist parades: the small feeder parades and competitive band parades. Band parades have been growing in popularity in recent years and probably do account for a part of the overall increase, but it is unlikely that they count for most of it. Instead it is likely that an increasing number of feeder parades are held prior to the main events. In talking with members of the loyal orders it is apparent that many Orangemen may be involved in three or more parades on anniversaries such as the Twelfth. First parading from a Master's house to the hall, then from the hall to the transport, then perhaps at a district assembly point before arriving at the main venue. Each parade would require separate permission. Duplicated among the hundreds of lodges on parade on the Twelfth, this process would boost the total numbers dramatically. It has also been suggested that the police may class the outward and return legs of a parade as two parades in the same way as the residents of the lower Ormeau Road area, whereas Orangemen would regard the outward and return route as a single parade. Some of the increase may be due, therefore, to differing interpretations as to what constitutes a parade.

5.3 Republican Parades
It should be noted that, over the period from 1992 to 1994, the average number of Republican parades has also steadily increased, whereas it had remained stable over the previous two periods. This increase was sustained in 1995.

There are three groups within the nationalist community which hold regular parades, the Ancient Order of Hibernians (AOH), the Irish National Foresters (INF) and the republican movement. The Hibernians and the Foresters are similar in organisational structure to the loyal orders and both have their origins in the brotherhoods and Friendly Societies which were popular in the nineteenth century. Both were also prominent in the nationalist campaign for Home Rule in the 1880-1914 period and were prominent in maintaining a nationalist tradition of parading during the Stormont years. They have been eclipsed by the republican movement in this area since the beginning of the Troubles. The AOH hold their main parades on St Patrick's Day (17 March), and on Lady Day (15 August). These are often held in smaller towns and villages but in recent years they have paraded in Derry, Downpatrick and Newry. The INF hold their annual parade in early August usually in County Armagh or County Down. Both organisations also hold a number of local church parades and occasional banner unfurling ceremonies. The main anniversaries would attract about 15 bands and divisions (the largest recent parade in Derry in 1995 drew 33 bands) and they would therefore be classed as small by the standards of loyalist parades.

The republican movement has become more prominent in holding commemorative parades, the Easter Rising being the main anniversary with numerous parades held on Easter Sunday across Ireland. Under Stormont, Easter parades in the north were often stopped and at best were confined to strongly nationalist areas, but some form of public commemoration was usually held. Since the Troubles republicans have established major parades to mark the anniversaries of Bloody Sunday - the end of January in Derry; the Hunger Strikes - early May in Belfast; and Internment - early August in Belfast. Smaller annual commemorative parades are held elsewhere in the north, particularly to honour the local IRA volunteers.

Some of the increase, in what the RUC classify as Republican parades, is probably due to this growing number of commemorations to the republican dead; but another part is probably due to the increased confidence and determination of nationalist and republican groups to claim their rights to parade and hold public rallies in major centres. It was only in 1993 that the annual Internment Commemoration in August was allowed to parade into Belfast city centre and hold its rally in front of the City Hall. The same year, the Ancient Order of Hibernians held their first ever parade in the city of Derry. The city has long had one of the largest AOH Divisions but during the Troubles the organisation had been reluctant to parade there for fear of provoking violence. This desire to parade in the neutral commercial centres of towns with a substantial nationalist population, underpinned the disputes in Castlederg and Lurgan in the period under consideration.

5.4 Summary
While much of the emphasis has been placed on the significance of tradition and traditional parades, the statistical material published by the RUC suggests that this is not enough to explain the significance of parading in the popular culture of Northern Ireland. While long standing parades may form the basis of the annual cycle of the marching season, the

steady but persistent increase in overall numbers indicates that parading is intimately related to contemporary concerns and is not simply indicative of a people trapped in their past.

Parades have always been a part of the broader political process in the north, even when they have been glossed as no more than religious or cultural events. This is not to suggest that they are not religious or cultural events but that the political dimension cannot be excluded. Northern Ireland has always been a deeply divided society; power and authority have not been equally shared, civil and political rights have not been equally shared, wealth and access to the sources of wealth have not been equally shared, and both working class Catholics and Protestants have suffered as a result. The right to parade has been an area in which one community has been favoured in relation to the other. Parading has long been a source of antagonism and has often served to increase tension, and sometimes to generate conflict, in a number of areas. In the past parades have often served as a surrogate for low level warfare and, with the arrival of the ceasefires in 1994, the issue of parades became a prominent and highly visible means of displaying and mobilising behind traditional political demands in an alternative site of conflict. In 1995 the Troubles continued, to the sound of the beating drum and marching feet.

PART 2

SECTION 6: PARADES IN CONFLICT DURING 1995

This section offers a chronological overview of the major disputes involving parades in 1995. Although the background focus of the report has been on loyalist parades, this overview includes all the parades, both loyalist and republican, that were contested, or provoked trouble, during the year. If one is trying to obtain a fuller picture of the events of the year, and attempting to show how one dispute can affect another, then it is impossible to ignore any part of the equation. For analysis we have divided the 1995 parading year into four distinct periods:

> *Period One*, discussed in this section, includes the build up to the beginning of the marching season at Easter, and the first parades, which are mostly small and localised events, in April and May.
> *Period Two*, discussed in Section Seven, focuses on the main Orange Order parades which begin in June and continue until the Twelfth of July. This is an intense period especially in the immediate build up to the Twelfth itself. After the Twelfth there is a break in the main parading calendar until marching recommences in late July.
> *Period Three*, discussed in Section Eight, discusses the period from the end of July until the Apprentice Boys parade on 12 August. This event marks a second climax to the marching season.
> *Period Four*, discussed in Section Nine, considers the period from late August until the end of October which again is marked by many smaller parades, but also includes many of the parades organised by the Royal Black Institution.

Finally, in Section Ten, there is a summary overview of the events which links them back to some of the themes addressed earlier in this report.

Connecting all the events of 1995 were the parades that were planned to go along the lower Ormeau Road in Belfast. In all 14 parades were disputed on the small stretch of the road between the Ormeau Bridge and Donegall Pass. Twelve of these were loyalist parades (eight organised by the Orange Order, two by the Apprentice Boys and two by the Black Institution), and two were organised by republican groups. Only two parades were allowed to pass along the route: on the Twelfth of July and on the anniversary of the Relief of Derry. The dispute on the Ormeau Road did not generate a major reaction on the scale of the events that occurred at Drumcree in July and in Derry in August; it was a more localised and less symbolically powerful dispute. However, without the persistence of the Ormeau Road dispute over the conflicting 'rights to parade' and 'rights not to suffer parades' it is doubtful whether the major disputes would have developed and been managed in the way they did.

This chronology has been written from two principal sources. The first source of information has been the extensive reports in the local press in Northern Ireland (BT - Belfast Telegraph; IN - Irish News; NL - Newsletter; SL - Sunday Life; SW - Sunday World). The second source has been personal attendance at many of the disputed parades throughout the 1995 marching season. This afforded the opportunity for conversations with many of those either parading or protesting. Such conversations are not identified explicitly, some were brief, others continued over a range of such events. Further clarification of certain details has been made at subsequent interviews.

6.1 Background to the Ormeau Road dispute

On Saturday 18 February 1995, members of the Lower Ormeau Concerned Committee (LOCC) put up a series of mock road signs, indicating 'No Orangemen on this road', on lamp posts along a stretch of the lower Ormeau Road. This move graphically relaunched the public campaign to have loyalist parades re-routed away from the lower Ormeau area. A campaign which had begun in March 1992 after five people were killed by the UFF in a bookmakers shop on the lower Ormeau the previous month.

The lower Ormeau had formerly been a Protestant area, and the mini-Twelfth parade incorporated the once continuous loyalist communities of Ballynafeigh, Ormeau Road and Donegall Pass on its circuit. However, population movements during the Troubles have meant that the lower Ormeau area is now a nationalist area. The loyalist parades were no longer as welcome as they once were, and even before the events of 1992 they had provoked protests by residents.

At the 1992 parade, nationalist protesters were confined to side streets to allow the parade to pass by. As the Orangemen passed the bookmakers shop a number of those marching made disrespectful five-fingered gestures and taunts to the protesters. These actions were widely seen on television and provoked widespread outrage. The Northern Ireland Secretary, Sir Patrick Mayhew, stated that their behaviour would have "disgraced a tribe of cannibals" (IN 11-7-92). The Orange Institution acted swiftly and disciplined a number of individuals, but gave no publicity to this. The following year, after some pressure from the RUC, the mini-Twelfth parade was voluntarily re-routed so that it did not cross over the Ormeau Bridge; instead, it went up the road and around the Rosetta area.

After the events of 1992, residents from the lower Ormeau area formed the LOCC with the single aim of having all loyalist parades re-routed away from the lower Ormeau Road. In 1994, protesters tried unsuccessfully to stop the Twelfth feeder parade along the road, and clashed with police as they protested against a Reformation Day parade in October. This led to decision to make a more concerted attempt to stop the parades in 1995 (BT 12-7-94).

The appearance of the road signs in February 1995 brought an angry response from Belfast County Grand Master of the Orange Order, Robert Saulters, who called them both 'provocative' and 'offensive'. He demanded that the authorities remove the signs within 48 hours, while rejecting calls for Orange Order to keep out of lower Ormeau area (SL 19-2). The Grand Master of the Orange Institution, Martin Smyth, claimed that only a small group of people were against the parades and the majority of the Catholic community had no problems with Orange parades along the Ormeau Road. He said that the "real problem there has been the advent of people who are developing the Nazi fascist approach of ghettoism" (IN 7-3).

Some effort was made to resolve the dispute before the first parade, which was due on Easter Monday, but there was no real progress. The issue was raised at a general community meeting organised by a group called the Peace Committee held at the Ballynafeigh Community Hall on 18 January, at which members of the Lower Ormeau Residents Action Group (LORAG) were present. The Peace Committee offered to act as intermediaries. This offer was conveyed to the LOCC who felt that it "would be a waste of time" and instead they proposed holding face to face talks with the Orangemen to try to reach an agreement. The Orangemen ruled out any direct contact at this time. An acrimonious exchange of letters in the press, in which each side accused the other of failing to respond to overtures, illustrated the distance between the two sides (SL 26-2, 5-3, IN 8-3, BT 15-3).

In mid-April, as the first parade approached, relatives of those killed in the bookmakers shop issued a letter to the marchers which was later published in the *Andersonstown News* (15-4):

We, the relatives of those murdered and injured in the attack on Sean Graham's bookmakers, wish to make the following plea to the Orange Order, the Black Preceptory and the Apprentice Boys.

We are making this appeal at this time as we feel the situation has gone on too long. What we are asking is quite simple; we are asking that these organisations find alternative routes for their marches which avoid the Lower Ormeau.

We are asking for this because we feel it will make a great contribution to the peace process, but more importantly it will allow us and our families to get on with our lives without the tension and fear which these parades generate every year.

We are not seeking this from a spirit of revenge or malice, but because we believe these parades are a serious hindrance to the reconciliation which we all seek. We do not wish to impose our views on anyone, nor to restrict people's right to express their culture in whatever way they wish. All we ask is that they take the views and feelings of others into consideration while they do so.

We hope the Orange Order etc. can accept this and also that they will accept it when we tell them that their parades over the past three years have caused deep hurt to us and our families. We hope that they will now end that hurt.

This letter produced a reply from Ballynafeigh District late in May which was not made public.

6.2 Easter: The marching season begins
The issue was brought to a head for the first time when the Belfast Branch of the Walker Club of the Apprentice Boys was prevented from parading along the Ormeau Road on Easter Monday, 17 April. They had planned to follow their normal route to meet other Belfast branches at Linenhall Street, before taking a bus to the main parade in Ballymoney. About 200 protesters gathered at the Ormeau Bridge, and the RUC forced the Apprentice Boys and their band to board their bus on Annadale Embankment, in order to prevent "serious public disorder". William Oliver, treasurer of the local Apprentice Boys club said: "Our civil rights have been violated. We have walked along this route for 90 odd years and we are not breaking the law". The Governor of the Apprentice Boys, Alistair Simpson, claimed that the RUC decision to re-route the parade had turned the clock back two decades and had raised tension both among

Protestants on the Ormeau Road and among the Apprentice Boys (NL 18-4-95). Local politicians were also quick to offer their opinions on the issue. Ian Paisley had already protested to the RUC at mere rumours that the parade was to be re-routed. Chris McGimpsey (UUP) accused the RUC of "caving in" to the demonstrators, and Jim Rodgers (UUP) described the protest as part of a co-ordinated Sinn Fein plan to disrupt Orange parades throughout the summer. Philip McGarry (All) pointed out that as the main parade was being held in Ballymoney, there was no need to parade along the Ormeau Road, and the Sinn Fein representative, Sean Hayes, welcomed the decision and called for the re-routing of Orange parades from nationalist areas across Ulster (BT 13-4, 20-4, NL 19-4-95). These positions were to be repeated throughout the summer.

The first Orange parade, to a charity service in the Ulster Hall, was due along the Ormeau Road on Sunday, 23 April. In the preceding week, LOCC argued that it was irresponsible for the RUC to leave the issue unresolved until just before the parade was due. They claimed that this only served to increase tension and raise the risk of confrontation. Gerard Rice, spokesperson for LOCC, said that they did not want any trouble at the parade and if there was a disturbance it would be due to the police failing to make a decision early enough. This argument was to be put on a number of occasions through the summer. Assistant Chief Constable Bill Stewart replied that a decision "could not be given at this stage", but appealed for "good will and common sense" (BT 20-4, 22-4, IN 22-4).

On Sunday 23 April, an estimated 600 people blocked the Ormeau Bridge three hours before the parade arrived. The police informed the protest organisers that the parade was being re-routed just five minutes before it was due at the bridge. ACC Bill Stewart said the decision was taken "in the interests of maintaining the peace". The 60 Orangemen, accompanied by 150 supporters carrying a banner stating "Ballynafeigh - No to Rerouting", were met by a wall of police Land Rovers at the bridge. The Orangemen refused to take an alternative route to the Ulster Hall, and instead held an impromptu service where they stood. Robert Saulters said that parity of esteem did not seem to apply to the Orangemen, pointing out that the organisers had deliberately not booked a band, in order to try "to accommodate the residents by walking quietly and reverently" but this appeared to have had no effect on the RUC decision (NL, IN 24-4). ACC Stewart denied that the RUC decision meant that there would be no further Orange parades along the road, but affirmed that "each parade is judged on its individual merits" (NL 24-4). In a later statement he added:

The lower Ormeau issue sums up in many ways the problem facing all of us. There are people with deeply-held convictions about their right to march peacefully. There are other people with equally firmly-held views that such marches are offensive. If we as a community accept that both traditions have a valid viewpoint, then surely the time has come to face up to the fact.

Following the re-routing of the parade, Ian Paisley had another meeting with senior RUC officers. He claimed the decision to stop the parades was political and was influenced by the government in Dublin. He also noted that the decision only encouraged people "to come out on the streets and to threaten violence and a breach of the peace in order to stop legally constituted parades and events. The clear lesson that will be drawn from the police action is that it pays to have mob rule". Ian Paisley Jr. added that "the people who sit down in the road were the lawbreakers, not the people attempting to pass through the area" (BT 25-4, NL 25-4, 3-5).

6.3 VE Day and other Belfast parades
Two parades were due to pass along the Ormeau Road at the beginning of May. Ballynafeigh Orangemen planned to join the VE Day commemorations outside City Hall on 4 Thursday, and a Sinn Fein parade was planned to leave the lower Ormeau area to walk to the Falls Road for the Hunger Strike commemorations on 7 Sunday. In the build-up the newspapers reported that tension was rising in the area and that confrontation was expected at both parades (BT 3-5, NL 1-5, 3-5).

A new residents group, ACORD (A Community Organisation's Response to Despotism), based on the Donegall Pass, announced that they planned to block the republican parade in retaliation against the campaign to stop Orange parades. Sinn Fein responded by announcing that it would voluntarily re-route their march along the Ormeau because of the ongoing protests by LOCC and the opposition from ACORD. Sinn Fein also called on the Orangemen voluntarily to re-route parades and to begin talks with LOCC (IN 3-5). ACORD went ahead with the protest and blocked the junction of the Ormeau Road and Donegall Pass. The protest was addressed by community leaders and William Smith of the Progressive Unionist Party (PUP).

An attempt to hold a last minute meeting between the RUC, LOCC and the Orangemen, to try to resolve the issue of the VE Day parade, failed. Once again the RUC blocked the parade at the Ormeau Bridge and once again the Orangemen held a service in front of the police cordon. District Chaplain, The Reverend William Hoey, warned that "while we are a law abiding people and support the forces of law and order, we may be pushed too far". Gerard Rice, LOCC, again criticised the RUC tactics and warned that they could lead to a confrontation between loyalists and the police in the future. He said that while LOCC were willing to talk to the Orange Order, there should be no more parades until early July, and all future parades in the area should be re-routed. Michael McGimpsey (UUP) said LOCC had backed out of a meeting, which it was hoped would resolve the dispute over VE day, and he accused them of raising sectarian and communal tension by their protests. He suggested that their actions were "in danger of bringing us back to 1969 again". The LOCC claimed there was no offer of a meeting (BT 5-5, NL 5-5).

Although the Ormeau Road protest passed of peacefully on VE Day, there was serious rioting in east Belfast late in the evening, when an estimated 200 loyalists returning from the commemorations clashed with the RUC near the Short Strand. Petrol bombs were thrown at police in the Dee Street area and an off-license was looted (BT 5-5). Tom Haire, Belfast County Grand Secretary, said that in spite of these disturbances the rest of the marching season was not in any doubt, although he admitted that the Order would have to "review our stewarding". He said that there had been "an exceptionally big turn out" in Ballymacarrett, but "as far as I am aware none of our own membership ... was involved in anything". He said that there had been a lot of frustration when the Ballynafeigh District had been prevented from joining the VE Day service at the City Hall and suggested that if a resolution to the dispute on the Ormeau Road could be found it would take the heat out of the marching debate. He added that "when you consider the number of times that Orangemen have paraded that particular area (the Short Strand), there are very few incidents of the magnitude of last night". However, Joe O'Donnell (SF) said that the rioting had now raised the question of Orange parades in the area and "it is now time that the question of re-routing these sectarian marches away from the Short Strand area should be seriously looked at" (IN 6-5).

An editorial in the *Irish News* stated that "there is an onus on the RUC, Sinn Fein and organisers of loyalist parades to review their respective positions". It argued that the RUC should take a firm and binding decision on the Ormeau issue to prevent tension from rising and people from gathering on the streets before each proposed parade: "Many loyalists feel a sense of outrage when they are prevented from walking along a 'traditional' route for their demonstrations. However ... (the Orange Order) lost whatever rights they might have had to demonstrate on the Ormeau Road on the infamous night in July 1992." It suggested that Sir Patrick Mayhew and the RUC should announce that similar marches will no longer be allowed along the road, and, as with the Tunnel parade route in Portadown, loyalists would eventually accept that times have changed (IN 6-5).

Following the VE Day protests, residents in Suffolk demanded that the annual republican Hunger Strike march, from Twinbrook to the Falls, be re-routed away from the loyalist estate. One local woman said "We do not want any coat trailing by Republican IRA supporters past our estate. This is not a traditional parade and could do a lot of harm". An unnamed RUC officer said "This will be a nightmare summer over the parades issue" and another added "we could be in for a tit-for-tat blocking all over the place throughout the summer" (SL 7-5). Minutes before the parade set of, on Sunday 7 May, the RUC served a re-routing order on the organisers, and used 40 Land Rovers to keep marchers and protesters apart. After a 25 minute stand-off which involved a sit down protest, but no serious trouble, the marchers took an alternative route, along Suffolk Road and Doon Road, to the rally in Dunville Park. Sinn Fein councillor Anne Armstrong told the crowd: "This march has been going on a number of years ... there has never been a major incident and this march was always well stewarded. Nothing has been re-routed here since Bobby Sands funeral 14 years ago. We don't want to go back 14 years". Alex Maskey, (SF), claimed that the "decision has been dictated by the DUP and Orange Order, and has been taken simply because of Orange parades which have attracted publicity in recent weeks. Today is not intended to be offensive". However, John Hume urged Sinn Fein to rethink their policy of street demonstrations, while Steve McBride (All) accused the Sinn Fein of adopting "aggressive, confrontational and fundamentally sectarian" tactics on the issue (IN 8-5, NL 8-5). The following day, republicans were blamed for damage caused to 12 cars which were attacked in the Suffolk estate overnight. It was assumed that the attacks were in response to the re-routing of the earlier Hunger Strike parade (BT 8-5).

The RUC responded to the four days of parades, protests and violence, by restating their calls for calm and restraint and a spokesman warned against inflammatory predictions of "a long hot summer". In Dublin the Tanaiste, Dick Spring, suggested that there should be a halt to all parades in the north during the "so-called marching season", to encourage the peace process (IN 10-5). Labour's shadow Northern Ireland Secretary Marjorie Mowlam also announced that she would welcome a voluntary decision, by both communities, to abandon marches this year (NL 12-5). An editorial, in the *Belfast Telegraph*, agreed with Dick Spring that a moratorium on parades would help the peace process, but then added "his call stands no chance of being heeded ... (his) comments display a remarkable ignorance of the realities of life in NI. The best that can be hoped for is that organisers of parades and demonstrations show some sensitivity towards their neighbours" (BT 10-5). Unionist politicians had no sympathy for Spring's proposals. Nigel Dodds (DUP) had already claimed that the NIO was in collusion with Dublin in suppressing "traditional, peaceful and legal" Orange parades, while Ian Paisley Jr. said the Tanaiste's speech indicated "that the pan-nationalist front are attempting now to construct a climate where it will become illegal to express a cultural identity other than Irish nationalism". Martin Smyth said Orange marches were "not sectarian" and the Order would not surrender to "the bully boys" (NL 9-5, 11-5).

Later the same week it was reported that plans for face-to-face talks between the Ballynafeigh Orangemen and LOCC, which had been mediated by the Quakers, had broken down when the Orangemen objected to Gerard Rice being a member of the Ormeau delegation because he had been imprisoned for republican offences. The Orangemen said they would be happy to continue with the talks if Rice was replaced, but LOCC refused to change their delegation: they would not be dictated to by the Orangemen, and said that, after the scenes outside Sean Graham's in 1992, "it is not for them to now present this holier-than-thou attitude to us". Noel Liggett, District Secretary of Ballynafeigh LOL confirmed that they would not be prepared to meet with Gerard Rice, but he left the way open for a future meeting: "trust and respect have to be built up" he said. The *Irish News* editorial described the decision of the Orangemen as "deeply depressing", and the paper restated their opinion, first that the RUC should make a definite ruling on the issue of parades in the area, and second that future parades should only be allowed on the lower Ormeau with the agreement of all sections of the community (BT 12-5, IN 12-5, 13-5, NL 12-5, SL 14-5).

6.4 Disputes in Castlederg
While most attention was on the parade protests in Belfast there were disputes at three parades in Castlederg Co. Tyrone in the period between

30 April and 28 May. On the first occasion the RUC re-routed a march organised by Saoirse, a republican organisation which campaigns on the issue of prisoners. They had planned to parade from the nationalist Hillview estate, through the centre of the town and back to the estate, to publicise their campaign. However, the parade, which was due to take place on a Sunday afternoon, was re-routed in the morning because of the fear of "serious public disorder". When the marchers reached the police cordon they held a short sit-down protest in response before dispersing (NL 1-5). More serious trouble occurred a week later and two days after the rioting following the VE Day parades Belfast, on the evening of Saturday 6 May. This time there was trouble at the annual band parade of Castlederg Young Loyalists. Newspapers reported that, as the parade passed the Ferguson Crescent area, members of one of the leading bands broke ranks and clashed with a group of nationalists standing outside a bar. Police then intervened to keep the two sides apart. Two people were arrested and four RUC officers were injured. Councillor Thomas Kerrigan (DUP) complained of the "provocative flying of tricolours" in the area, while Councillor Charlie McHugh (SF) contrasted the recent re-routing of a Saoirse parade with the way police were willing to allow loyalist bands to parade through a nationalist area (SL 7-5, Tyrone Constitution 11-5).

The third dispute occurred three weeks later. After the Saoirse parade was banned in early May, a Nationalist Rights Committee was formed to take up the cause of access to the town centre for nationalist organisations. This group was permitted to hold a rally in the Diamond on Sunday 28 May when an estimated 1000 people paraded from the Hillview estate into the town centre. A number of loyalist protesters scuffled with the police but they were unable to prevent the rally from being held. Afterwards they held a short ceremony at the War Memorial, to reclaim it for themselves (An Phoblacht 1-6). As a result the nationalists felt they had achieved what they wanted and that they had established their right to parade in the town centre, but at the same time they did not push the issue and they did not hold any more parades during the year. Tension continued in the town, especially on parading days, and this eventually culminated in a night of street fighting which caused thousands of pounds worth of damage following the Last Saturday parades in August (Section 9.2).

6.5 Summary
The dispute over parading rights remained relatively low-key through the early weeks of the marching season. The main interest was on the Ormeau

Road, where the RUC appeared to have comfortably controlled the first three loyalist parades, none of which had been allowed along its intended route. However, warnings signs were clear. The police were regularly criticised for refusing to make a decision until the last minute which, it was claimed, only served to raise tension and bring people out on to the streets. The police replied that they could only re-route a parade if there was a threat of serious public disorder and this threat could only be judged by the number of people who came onto the street. The importance of this argument was not lost on Ian Paisley, who argued that this logic only led to mob rule. It would prove to be a significant factor in the escalation of the parading dispute in future months.

Furthermore, there was a small but perhaps significant difference between the police tactics adopted in Belfast and those adopted in Castlederg, which does indicate that there was some scope in policing strategy. In Belfast the decision to re-route the loyalist parades was always made at the last minute, whereas in Castlederg, the Saoirse parade on 30 April, was re-routed some hours before it was due to start. It could be argued that taking the decision earlier, rather than later, reduces the potential for conflict between the opposing groups because it attracts less people onto the streets and encourages the issue to be considered through force of argument rather than force of numbers. The police always acknowledged that they were not responsible for adjudicating the moral rights of a parade, merely responsible for policing matters. After the violence at the parades on the Ormeau in July and August, the remaining parades were re-routed several days in advance of the event and few people turned out to protest.

There were also early indications of the knock-on effect of parade disputes and the connections between various disputes. The rioting in the Short Strand on VE Day was attributed to anger among loyalists at the decision to prevent the Ballynafeigh Orangemen from parading to the main rally. The loyalist protests at republican parades on the Ormeau and at Suffolk were also in response to objections raised to Orange parades on the Ormeau.

Political figures were often ready with suitable sound bites, but few suggestions were made that did anything other than restate existing positions. Politicians from both sides pointed out that their parades did not intend to cause offence, unionists retreated behind the shield of tradition, while republicans emphasised the importance of equal rights. When suggestions were made as to how the broader issue of the right to march should be dealt with, they were either dismissed out of hand, as per Dick Springs's suggestion of a moratorium, or they were ignored. There was no broad debate on the issue, and even local level negotiations were proving difficult to arrange. Although attempts had been made to bring the parties to the dispute on the Ormeau Road together, these had not been fruitful. Suspicion and mistrust dominated public exchanges.

6.6 Possible Ways Forward
While negotiations between the main parties on the Ormeau Road remained at stalemate, a contrasting range of options had been suggested as possible ways to deal with the issue. An anonymous group of Belfast Orangemen, who felt that the Order had been pushed around too much, suggested that it was time to make a stand and assert their traditional rights, and if necessary, the entire Belfast Twelfth parade should walk along the Ormeau Road. Bishop Brian Hannon of Clogher, used the platform of the General Synod of the Church of Ireland to call for restraint from all sides at Orange parades. He said that the right to walk on every street had to be measured against the right of the community as a whole to be protected from murder and mayhem. Meanwhile Barry McElduff of Sinn Fein criticised an RUC decision to allow a loyalist parade through the predominately nationalist village of Pomeroy, and called for an independent commission to be set up which could deal impartially with applications to hold parades in disputed areas (SL 14-5, IN 16-5, NL 19-5).

These three possible means of resolving the disputes can be categorised as (1) No Compromise, (2) Voluntary Restraint and (3) External Adjudicator. They would be voiced repeatedly throughout the coming weeks by a variety of political figures. They formed the basis of strategies of action for different groups concerned with the issue. The active participants, both parade and protest organisers, tended to adopt the 'No Compromise' strategy; the media, the police and many politicians continued to appeal, usually unsuccessfully, to peoples' civil duty and for 'restraint.' The suggestion that there should be an 'external commission' to oversee protests was regularly restated but was largely ignored, both by those actively seeking to retain their traditional rights and by those seeking change. Both groups perhaps feared that they would be forced to compromise and therefore would be seen to lose out in some way.

Although versions of each of these options was repeated with regularity there was little if any impetus to find either a compromise or a working solution. The problem was largely left to those with most personal interest in the issue who were rarely willing to meet each other, let alone discuss possible compromises. The focus of attention was at the local level with little interest in what the effects the issue might have on a wider scale. Less involved parties uttered wise words but remained on the sidelines. While mutual tolerance was repeated, mantra-like, its meaning was interpreted in different ways. To unionist writers and representatives tolerance meant that residents should accept Orange parades as a cultural event, while for their nationalist counterparts tolerance meant that Orangemen should acknowledge the validity of the objections and re-route their parades. There was to be little movement from these entrenched positions.

SECTION 7: THE ORANGE MARCHES

7.1 From Belfast to Bellaghy and Back
In spite of a four week break in the parading calendar in Belfast, no agreement had been reached by the time that the fourth loyalist parade was due on Ormeau Road on Sunday 18 June. This parade was different from the previous three in so far as it involved Orangemen from the Sandy Row District Lodge whose return route from church included a short section of the Ormeau Road. The Orangemen planned to attend a service in All Saints Parish Church on University Street and to return to Sandy Row via the Ormeau Road and Donegall Pass. The secretary of the District Orange Lodge, Billy McBride, said that three different groups from the lower Ormeau area have said they want nothing to do with the protests and he added: "The parade has followed the same route, every year for 98 years. We are going to church and coming home from church and we don't see anything wrong with that" (SL 18-5).

The LOCC insisted that the parade be re-routed, and asked why it could not return from church by the outward route and thus avoid the Ormeau Road area entirely. LOCC claimed that the RUC regarded this parade as different from the others, because it would not pass Sean Graham's shop and it would only be on the Ormeau Road for five minutes. A spokesperson also said that they had been warned by the RUC that they could be arrested if they protested against this parade (IN 14-6, 15-6). The LOCC later said that the Orange Order had made a suggestion, via the Quakers, to re-route this parade if the Ballynafeigh District Twelfth parade was allowed through. However, the Orange Order quickly responded by denying that there had been any attempt to do a deal over parades (SL 18-5). Concern was also expressed about a leaflet which had been distributed in the lower Ormeau area in the days preceding the parade. The anonymous leaflet quoted a Biblical analogy for the current dispute in the story of the Amorite King Sihon. It pointed out that when Sihon refused the Israelites access through his land: "Israel smote him with the edge of the sword, and possessed his land". The leaflet continued "Their request was similar to that of the Ballynafeigh Orangemen" and claimed "too many roads and towns have been lost already". Noel Liggett, of Ballynafeigh LOL, said he did not know who was responsible for the leaflet and that another leaflet had been circulated which had criticised the Orangemen for negotiating with the LOCC (BT 16-5, IN 17-5).

On Sunday 18 May, about 200 protesters gathered on the Ormeau

Road as the Orangemen attended their service. As they left the church the Orangemen were informed by RUC that their return route had been changed and they would not be allowed onto the Ormeau Road. Two dozen Land Rovers were used to block University Street and despite furious protests and a symbolic march to confront the police lines, the 150 Orangemen and their two bands were forced to return along University Street. Lodge official Cecil Dunwoody claimed police had given in to a "gang of troublemakers who don't even live on the Ormeau Road" and the Belfast County Grand Master, Robert Saulters, said "Catholic objections have now reached the point of absurdity. The RUC may as well be Ulster's gardai". Gerard Rice responded that "The Orange Order have to realise they are unacceptable in this area". He called for a moratorium on all marches in the area for the remainder of the marching season, to give time to allow all sides to address the issues concerned. He also suggested that the Order could bring Orangeism into the area in a different form to show that it was not "simply sectarianism, bigotry and a coat trailing exercise" (BT 19-5, IN 19-5, NL 19-5).

On following Saturday, 24 June the focus of interest shifted to west Belfast. Between 100-200 nationalist demonstrators staged a sit-down protest at the junction of Ainsworth Avenue and Springfield Road to try to prevent the north Belfast mini-Twelfth parade from walking up the Springfield Road to the Whiterock Orange Hall. This area has long been an interface between the Falls and the Shankill and was divided by a peaceline early in the Troubles. In recent years the parade has been opposed by Sinn Fein, the SDLP and others from the nationalist community. Serious rioting broke out in the Shankill area in 1993 after a member of the UVF was killed by a grenade he was holding as the parade made its way along Ainsworth Avenue.

The parade of about 300 Orangemen and a dozen bands passed peacefully after intervention by Alex Maskey and Billy Hutchinson helped to calm fraying tempers. However, as the RUC removed the nationalist protesters to allow the parade to pass, one officer was stabbed in the back and one person was arrested. On the Shankill side, loyalist "hard men" blocked both sides of the road in Ainsworth Avenue and prevented people following the parade from getting near to the police lines at the peaceline. A spokesman said: "We didn't want any drunks or troublemakers getting down to the gates at the peaceline ... Any violence would be just the excuse the republicans wanted to try and justify their outrageous campaign to get marches rerouted". Sinn Fein said it was "reprehensible" that the parade should be allowed through a vulnerable nationalist area. Alex Attwood (SDLP) agreed that the Whiterock parade should be re-routed away from the Springfield Road and that residents had a right to protest if the parade were not re-routed. But he criticised both Sinn Fein and the RUC for the way the protests at the mini-Twelfth parade had been handled. He said it was up to the Orange Order, police, political leaders and residents to ensure that such confrontations were not repeated on the Twelfth or on the weeks leading up to it (SW 25-6, SL 25-6, IN 26-5, 27-5, NL 26-5, 27-5 Andersonstown News 1-7).

Opposition to parades was also being mobilised elsewhere. A newly formed group calling itself Bellaghy Concerned Residents said that it had met with senior RUC officers in a bid to prevent a mini-Twelfth parade in the village and that they would also protest against other forthcoming parades in the "80% nationalist village". In Portadown, the Garvaghy Road Residents Group, announced that they had asked for a meeting with the local Orange Order to request that they re-route two parades expected along the road in July. When they did not receive a response from the Orangemen, the residents issued a statement saying that they would hold a protest on 9 July as the first of these parades returned from Drumcree Church. At a press conference on 4 July, spokesperson Don Mercer confirmed that the protest would be peaceful and explained why it was necessary. He said that the during the parades nationalists "become virtual prisoners in their own area" and this "creates a siege mentality and our people no longer accept this". The parades "harken back to the days of power and privilege of the old Stormont regime" and "have more in common with the displays of fascism witnessed in Europe over 50 years ago than with any folk festival".

There was also speculation that organised protests at parades would spread more widely through Belfast. Councillor Jim Rodgers (UUP) suggested that nationalists might be planning to attempt to disrupt both a Somme parade in east Belfast and the main Twelfth parade itself in the city. Although there was no evidence to support this claim it was widely reported at the time and it was repeated at a later date. In response to the general raising of tension over parades the Mid-Ulster branch of the UVF and the Combined Loyalist Military Command in Belfast announced that they would be monitoring the issue in future weeks (BT 23-6, 29-6, 30-6 IN 8-6, SL 2-7, 5-7, Mid Ulster Observer 29-6, Portadown Times 30-6).

July began with a report in the *News Letter* that the RUC had drawn up contingency plans for an increase in confrontation in the run-up to the

Twelfth and this included a strengthening of Divisional Mobile Support Units. An editorial in the paper criticised, what it called the Sinn Fein 'rent-a-mob' tactics, and said "to some extent the Orange Order is caught in the middle as hardliners on both sides adopt a 'not an inch' approach to marches, which in a more enlightened society, ought to be able to take place without causing offence or disturbing the peace". While calling for 'tolerance on all sides' it said that republicans were being unreasonable in objecting to Orange parades which it insisted were "a colourful, cultural and above all peaceful procession" (NL 1-7). The same week, an editorial in the *Andersonstown News* argued for the need for talks between the organisers of parades and the residents "before these blood and thunder marches actually take place"; it continued: "Could both sides not develop the concept of an independent panel which would bring residents and march organisers together to discuss proposed routes and parades? Such a panel could draw up a marcher's charter which would lay down basic principles in the organising of parades and even select agreed neutral areas - outside the City Hall, for example - where parades should be encouraged" (AN 1-7). These two editorials again illustrate the gap between the thinking on the unionist and the nationalist sides. The unionists continued to insist that all protests were a Sinn Fein front and that nationalists were being unreasonable and intolerant in objecting to peaceful parades. They did not accept that the objections of residents were in any way genuine. While the nationalist position argued that there should be face to face discussion over the issues, it ignored or disbelieved the importance of parades as a local cultural event for the loyalist community. Each side could therefore, safely ignore the other's position as being unrealistic.

With three parades due along the Ormeau Road in the first two weeks of July the protests looked certain to continue and possibly escalate, when Ballynafeigh District Lodge rejected proposals to resolve the issue put forward by LOCC. Their package proposed an 18-month suspension of all parades, loyalist and nationalist, along the lower Ormeau, but it would allow the Twelfth parade to go through, and other parades could pass as long as they had the mutual agreement of both sides. LOCC also said that they would be prepared to host photographic displays and debates either about Orangeism or involving Orange Order representatives, to further mutual understanding. Gerard Rice said "the parade organisers must take into account the feelings of the residents of the areas the parade will pass through" but he also agreed that "we as a community have a responsibility to look beyond past hurts to recognise the potential for improved future relationships". He confirmed that the Orange Order had made their own proposals under which they would retain all their traditional parades but they would not ask for any new ones. Rice said that these proposals were unacceptable to LOCC and, although, negotiations had broken down, LOCC was open to further talks. The Ballynafeigh Orangemen in turn rejected the proposals made by the LOCC, which they said were "pure blackmail". They added that community relations could not be improved through the repression of a legitimate expression of culture (IN 30-6).

The first of the three July parades, and the fourth from Ballynafeigh since Easter, was held on Sunday 2 July. The Orangemen planned to parade to a Somme memorial service but were again stopped at the Ormeau Bridge by the RUC. Some 300 protesters, including a number of Sinn Fein councillors had gathered on the lower Ormeau side of the bridge. The Orangemen held a short religious service at the bridge, and then returned to Ballynafeigh. In response to the blocking of the parade, George Dawson, a spokesman for the Independent Orange Order, called on Orange leaders to organise mass movements and diversionary tactics to help keep all parade routes open (IN 3-7, NL 3-7). ACORD held a meeting from 6.00 to 7.00 in the evening, and blocked off the Ormeau Road and Donegall Pass junction. A statement was read out to a local RUC Inspector. It stated that if the Protestant community of the Ormeau Road could not walk down the Ormeau Road to attend their place of worship then the Roman Catholic community of the Ormeau Road would not be allowed to walk down the road to attend their service at St. Malachy's Church, Alfred Street.

Three days later, on Wednesday 5 July, with widescale disturbances and violence in nationalist areas of Belfast and elsewhere following the release of Lee Clegg on 3 July, the first violence erupted on the Ormeau Road. Ironically, the mini-Twelfth parade was not intended to cross the bridge since it had been voluntarily re-routed after the events in 1992. However, at the junction of Annadale Embankment and the Ormeau Road, a number of the bands made a gesture to turn to cross the bridge before continuing their march in the opposite direction up to the Orange hall. These actions encouraged a number of loyalist supporters, who were following the parade, to attack the police lines blocking the bridge. The violence was short lived, however, involving only a small percentage of those present. A few demonstrators climbed on the police vehicles and waved flags at the residents of the lower Ormeau area. A few bottles and other missiles were thrown, but the events scarcely justified the inflammatory front page headlines in the *News Letter* which described it as the 'Battle on the Bridge'. Eleven police and two civilians were injured, 10 RUC Land Rovers were damaged and 4 people were arrested at the clashes (BT 6-7, NL 6-7).

There were also clashes in Bellaghy the same night where "rival factions traded insults as loyalist bands paraded through part of the 80% nationalist town". Members of Bellaghy Concerned Residents had gathered a petition signed by the representatives of 200 local householders, and had met with senior local police officers in a bid to have a mini-Twelfth parade, organised by the local Orange Lodge, banned from the village. When this failed to have any effect they planned to hold a sit down demonstration on the parade route, but the RUC issued a banning order on the protest shortly before the parade was due to start. Forty RUC Land Rovers and over 200 police were called in to control the events and the protesters were confined to the sides of the road. Forty bands paraded through the village during the evening. Five people were arrested as missiles and insults were exchanged by republicans and loyalists (BT 6-7, Mid-Ulster Observer 29-6, 13-7).

In the run up to the Twelfth and with tension and speculation mounting, the focus of media attention remained on the Ormeau Road and in particular on how the Orangemen would react to the threat of re-routing. Statements and rumours issued from various levels of the organisation. The local Orangemen insisted that they would continue to follow their traditional parade route. The Ballynafeigh District Orangemen reaffirmed that they considered that the package offered by the LOCC, to allow the Twelfth of July parade through on condition that there were no more parades through the area until the end of 1996, was "pure blackmail". Speculation continued that the Ormeau Road would be the site of a major Orange demonstration on the Twelfth. Some rank and file members were demanding that all nine Belfast districts should converge on the Ormeau Road in protest at police tactics to block parades. They suggested that because it was the beginning of the holiday period: "Thousands of Orangemen could stand there for days if necessary to prove our point". Belfast County Secretary, Tom Haire, said the Orange Order were not ruling out taking 20,000 marchers down the Ormeau Road on the Twelfth: "We are monitoring the situation from day to day". In turn the Grand Orange Lodge of Ireland accused the RUC of giving in to an orchestrated campaign to deny the legitimate expression of Orange culture. The RUC "have allowed the threat of republican violence to be used to prevent peaceful legal parades along traditional routes" they said in a statement. There was also speculation that the Order was planning to take the RUC to the Ulster High Court to ensure they would be allowed to walk down the Ormeau Road on the Twelfth. Amidst such speculation, a *Sunday World* editorial argued that it was time for the Orange leaders, "James Molyneaux, MP, Martin Smyth, MP, and the likes of Willie Ross, MP - Orangemen all - to tell their members to respect the rule of law and order". It said that the politicians should be in Portadown that day, and at the Ormeau Bridge on the Twelfth, and tell their members "to respect and obey the RUC" (BT 6-7, NL 7-7, IN 8-7, SW 9-7). There was no response from the unionist political leadership.

7.2 The Siege of Drumcree
While most attention remained trained on the Ormeau Road, the Orangemen's frustration at what they perceived to be the constant attacks on their culture and traditions erupted in Portadown on Sunday 9 July. Portadown has long been perceived as the heartland of Orangeism but in the past decade parades through the nationalist Tunnel and Obins Street area had been vigorously opposed by residents. As a result of the protests, all Orange parades had been re-routed from the area after 1986. Some were sent down Charles Street but the parade on the Twelfth morning was sent down the Garvaghy Road; as this was also a predominately nationalist area this change provoked opposition. Initially this was co-ordinated by the Drumcree Faith and Justice Group but in 1995 the protest was organised by the Garvaghy Road Residents Group who included representatives from a wide range of local organisations.

When members of the Portadown District left Drumcree Church at midday, they were advised by the RUC that their safety could not be guaranteed if they paraded along the Garvaghy Road, where 300 residents were staging a street protest. Rather than take an alternative route back into town, or dispersing at Drumcree, the Orangemen decided to wait where they were, until they were able to follow their traditional route back into town. It soon became clear to the Orangemen that the police were planning neither to clear the protesters nor to force the parade through, but they determined to remain where they were until allowed along the Garvaghy Road. As the stand off continued through the afternoon and evening, the numbers of Orangemen and supporters at Drumcree swelled. At the same time, demonstrations of support were displayed elsewhere: there were gatherings and protests in a number of other towns, and calls were made for a mammoth show of support in Portadown on the evening of 10 Monday, if the issue had not been resolved. Local MP, David Trimble, who had been at Drumcree for the service, announced: "I am here supporting the right of Portadown District to march their traditional route, the route they have taken for the last 188 years". Ian Paisley donned his Apprentice Boys collarette and arrived late on Sunday evening to negotiate with the police, claiming as his mandate his position as an MEP. However, ACC Freddie Hall insisted that the Orangemen had only two choices: to disperse at Drumcree and go home, or walk back the route they had come (BT 10-7, IN 10-7, NL 10-7).

The stand off continued through Monday. Tension increased as thousands of Orangemen and supporters arrived for the rally in the evening. They occupied the fields around Drumcree Church while thousands more supporters occupied the streets of Portadown. Ian Paisley was one of the main speakers at the rally, he insisting that: "There can be no turning back on this issue - we will die if necessary rather than surrender". While large numbers of Orangemen listened to the speeches, elsewhere some of the Orangemen and supporters were getting restless and tried to break through the police lines. The RUC responded to the assault by the crowd with plastic bullets. The *News Letter* headline the next day call it the "Battle of Drumcree". Eventually, after extensive discussion and mediation, involving the Orangemen, led by Paisley and Trimble, the Garvaghy Road residents, and the RUC, the Portadown Orangemen were allowed to parade down Garvaghy Road on Tuesday morning. Under the `agreement' only the local Portadown District Orangemen were allowed to walk the route and David Trimble and Ian Paisley met them at the town end of the road. The parade was quiet as there were no bands accompanying them, although this was because the bandsmen had gone home to change rather than part of any agreement, according to officers of Portadown District LOL. The Garvaghy Road residents lined the route to make a silent protest (see Jones et. al. 1995 for the Orange Order's discussion of these events).

Brendan McAllister, of the Mediation Network, said an agreement had been reached whereby the church parade would be allowed to complete its route, on condition that the Twelfth feeder parade, the following day, would take another route. However, David Trimble immediately disagreed with this understanding. He said "there is certainly no agreement by the District Lodge to reroute the Twelfth parade". While Trimble denied any compromise had been made, RUC ACC Freddie Hall also stated that the Orange Order would not be marching down Garvaghy Road on the Twelfth morning. The RUC also praised the Mediation Network for their work in helping to resolve the issue (IN 12-7, NL 12-7).

At the same time as the rally began at Drumcree on Monday evening, all major roads into the port of Larne were blockaded by Orangemen in support of the men in Portadown. Protests in solidarity were made in a number of towns and villages during the 'siege at Drumcree' but those in Larne had the most impact because of the disruption caused to trade and tourists. Articulated lorries were used to block the main Belfast to Larne road and bonfires were built in the middle of others. The blockade caused huge tail backs of traffic which extended for several miles. East Antrim MP Roy Beggs said he "wholeheartedly" supported the protest, which he claimed was peaceful but many freight businesses and travellers were not so happy at the events. Ferries sailed largely empty from the port. However, the police failed to clear the blockade, and it was only lifted on Tuesday morning, when the dispute in Portadown had been resolved (IN 11-7, 12-7, Larne Gazette 13-7).

7.3 Agreement on the Ormeau?

While attention switched to Portadown, negotiations continued to try to resolve the immediate issue of the parade along the Ormeau Road. An agreement between the Orange Order, the Royal Black Institution and the LOCC appeared to have been reached late in the evening on Monday 10, as a result of mediation by the Quakers. This agreement, which was witnessed by representatives of the RUC and by members of the Quakers, consisted of a preamble and five clauses:

> The Ballynafeigh District Orange Lodge believes in democracy and in everyone's right to enjoy civil and religious liberty. This means that all sections of the community must be free to express their religious and cultural traditions. The Lower Ormeau Concerned Community likewise accepts that all have a right to express their religious and cultural identity. Both parties, however, recognise that, in the exercise of these rights, all sides must be sensitive to the wishes and concerns of others. It will take time for the deep wounds suffered by many living along the whole of the Ormeau Road to heal; both parties are committed to assist that process.
>
> Accordingly the Lower Ormeau Concerned Community and the Ballynafeigh District Orange Lodge agree that:

1. The Ballynafeigh District Orange Lodge will walk down the entire length of the Ormeau Road on the morning of 12th July 1995.
2. The Ballynafeigh Black Preceptory will walk down the entire length of the Ormeau Road on the morning of 26th August 1995.
3. In future, parades of any description will take place along any part of the Ormeau Road between the Ormeau bridge and the railway bridge only where agreement has been made beforehand between the parade organisers and the people of the lower Ormeau Road. Only an open, public meeting of Lower Ormeau residents can give such agreement on behalf of the people of the Lower Ormeau Road.
4. The Lower Ormeau Concerned Community and the Ballynafeigh District Orange Lodge will either initiate or strongly support moves to improve appreciation and understanding of the culture and traditions of the people living on the Upper and Lower Ormeau Road.
5. This agreement has been satisfactorily verified in the presence of the Quaker representatives and representatives of the RUC.

However, after the events at Portadown and during a radio interview, Gerard Rice requested further confirmation of Clause 3 from Robert Saulters (County Grand Master of Belfast), in order to reassure the residents of the lower Ormeau that the agreement would be honoured. Rice said that the appearance of the Ballynafeigh Orange banner at Drumcree, meant the LOCC could not trust the Orangemen without further confirmation and, with no confirmation forthcoming, he felt the agreement had collapsed. Robert Saulters, speaking for the Ballynafeigh District, responded by saying that he had no intention of clarifying any part of the agreement. Two public meetings were then held among residents of the lower Ormeau. At the second meeting a consensus was reached to hold a protest with the aim of blocking the planned parade (IN 12-7, NL 12-7).

The *Sunday World* (16-7) later claimed the breakdown of the agreement was for three reasons:

1. A video shown at a meeting of lower Ormeau residents showed the Ballynafeigh banner at Drumcree.
2. Statements made by Ian Paisley and David Trimble at Drumcree, and the rioting during the protest, affected peoples attitude.
3. Sinn Fein objected to agreement at the last minute, because they felt it would show the RUC in too good a light.

Members of the LOCC have confirmed the importance of the Ballynafeigh banner at Portadown and the attitude of Paisley and Trimble in the failure of the residents of the lower Ormeau to confirm the agreement but they also emphasised the refusal of Ballynafeigh Orange lodge to publicly accept the third clause. These they felt were the key elements in the breakdown in the discussions.

On the Twelfth itself, there was a good deal of uncertainty as to what might happen at both the Garvaghy Road and on the lower Ormeau. In the end the parades in Portadown passed off peacefully. The eight Portadown country lodges and their accompanying bands "voluntarily" re-routed themselves away from the nationalist Garvaghy Road area. District officers have said that this decision was taken by the lodges concerned only on the Twelfth morning after they had assembled at Corcrain Orange Hall and discussed the matter among themselves. Their traditional route into town had been along Obins Street, rather than the Garvaghy Road, so when they left the hall the men walked a short distance along the Dungannon Road, as a symbolic gesture to tradition. They then made a U-turn and paraded via Charles Street to Carlton Street where they joined the main body of Portadown lodges. The District lodge issued a statement insisting that the re-routing had been undertaken voluntarily and that there had been no compromise deal agreed on Tuesday (NL 13-7).

On the lower Ormeau Road, the RUC decided to allow the Orangemen to join the main body of the parade at the City Hall. The nationalist residents were hemmed in to the side streets by up to 500 RUC officers wearing riot gear so that "a few dozen Orangemen" could parade along the road. Supporters of the Orangemen were stopped at the bridge, and not allowed to walk with them. The parade itself, passed "peacefully" despite noisy protests by the residents, but after the Orangemen had passed by the residents staged a sit-down protest in the road which lasted until the evening. The returning Orange parade was diverted away from the lower Ormeau by the police and the Orangemen walked via Botanic Avenue, Agincourt Avenue and the Stranmillis Embankment before crossing the Ormeau Bridge. Martin Smyth said he was pleased that the Ballynafeigh lodges had been allowed to parade their traditional route. But Gerard Rice of LOCC complained that the residents had been placed under curfew for the day. This theme was taken up by Gerry Adams (SF), who said that there was a direct comparison between the events at Drumcree and the Ormeau Road: "It has to do with that triumphalistic element of Orangeism which wants to show the Catholics in that area that the Orangemen are still in charge". In explaining their decision to allow the parade to follow its traditional route and the apparent change in tactics, the RUC said that the parade was permitted because of the ambiguity in the agreement between LOCC and the Orange Order. A police spokesman said the as LOCC had given a public assurance that there would be no violence at their protest, there was, therefore, "no likelihood of public disorder". He added that "the Orange Order said that they had agreed to all the conditions regarding future parades, and while the local community organisation did not reject the agreement, they expressed concern as to whether they could trust the Orange lodge". He also explained that the six previous parades, which had been re-routed had been local events whereas the Twelfth parade "a major event" and "if the parade had been re-routed, it could have had an effect everywhere in Northern Ireland" (IN 13-7, NL 13-7).

Although the LOCC rejected, or at least questioned, the validity of the agreement, the RUC acted as if it were still binding on all parties. Accordingly the police accepted the insistence of the LOCC that they would not provoke any violence, whereas at the previous parades it had been the threat of "serious public disorder" that had led to parades being re-routed. This may explain why the Twelfth parade was allowed through and why several subsequent parades would be re-routed some days before the event, whereas the pre-Twelfth parades were only re-routed at the last minute. The RUC continued to work to the terms of the agreement: future parades except those specified would only take place within a broad consensus. This strategy might work up to a point, but it failed to take into consideration the position of the Apprentice Boys, who were not party to the agreement and therefore were not constrained by its terms. Their parade was subject to differing policing considerations, which were related to events in Derry. The violence that would occur on that day appears to have been instrumental in encouraging the Black Preceptory to cancel their parade on the last Saturday, which would have been allowed under the July agreement.

In Dublin, both the Irish government and Fianna Fail leader Bertie Ahern expressed concern with the way in which the RUC appeared to have taken sides on the Ormeau Road in contrast to the more even handed approach adopted at Portadown. Fine Gael MEP, John Cushnahan, a former leader of the Alliance Party, repeated the call for the establishment of an independent commission to oversee any parade disputes. He said there was a need for a quasi-judicial body whose decisions would be binding to avoid an annual repetition of the recent events. Shadow Northern Ireland Secretary, Marjorie Mowlam, said it was necessary to build trust between the two communities and broker some form of community agreement before the next flash point arose (BT 13-7).

7.4 Arson and Vandalism

Although the other Twelfth parades passed peacefully, residents in the Short Strand area of east Belfast claimed they had been stoned by loyalists on the way back from the parade. Police admitted that they had fired several plastic bullets during the trouble and four officers had been injured. Joe O'Donnell (SF) called for all Orange parades to be moved away from the nationalist area because of violence following this parade and the rioting after the VE Day parade. He suggested the marchers should be re-routed along the Sydenham by-pass instead of using the Newtownards Road (BT 13-7, IN 14-7).

There was also an escalation of sectarian arson attacks and vandalism, which had begun in the run up to the Twelfth and now continued in the days following the parades. One of the earliest reported incidents had been on the evening of 1 July, when a Roman Catholic Church in Killyleagh, County Down, had a number of windows smashed, some hours after a loyalist Somme parade had passed through the village. It was the second attack on the church in a fortnight and it foreshadowed a spate of such attacks, on property belonging to both communities, over the next few weeks (IN 3-7). Between 11 July and 13 July Orange Halls in Belfast, Belleek, Dungannon, Keady, Rosslea and South Fermanagh were either damaged or destroyed. In the same few days a number of private houses and public buildings were also attacked, these included Catholic churches in Belfast, Cullybackey and Dundonald and the Protestant church at Drumcree. While these attacks were not directly linked to parades, they were clearly a result of the escalating tension that the disputes over parades had helped to generate. Sporadic attacks on Orange Halls continued through the remainder of July, but the intense wave of retaliatory attacks died away soon after the Twelfth, during the hiatus in the marching season (BT 18-7, NL 14-7, 20-7, 31-7).

However, the recommencement of the marching season in late July, was shadowed by a resumption of arson attacks which continued throughout August. An Orange Hall in Newtownhamilton, County Armagh, was badly damaged on 8 August, and Lambeg Orange Hall was gutted, a few days after the protests against the Apprentice Boys Relief of Derry parade erupted into violence. This was the twenty-first attack on Orange Halls in 1995. While there was widespread speculation at IRA involvement in the attacks, Sinn Fein denied any republican involvement and Councillor Annie Armstrong publicly called for an immediate end to all sectarian attacks on both property and individuals. Although the attacks ceased for a while there was another final round of damage in late August when the Corcrain Hall in Portadown and others near Lisburn and in Tyrone were damaged (BT 9-8, 15-8, 17-8, 19-8, 22-8, 30-8, IN 16-8, NL 17-8, 31-8).

7.5 Summary
As might have been expected, given the persistence of the parading disputes since Easter, July witnessed a dramatic increase in the scale of the problem. However, most people were probably surprised by the force of the reaction to the re-routing of the Drumcree Church parade. This surprise soon turned to concern, if not fear, as the dispute escalated and as numbers of people involved increased, especially as the Twelfth itself loomed large. For a short while, there seemed a real possibility that the whole thing could get out of hand. The crisis in Portadown focused people's minds and ensured a peaceful solution was reached, but it was only a short term and localised solution. The events at Drumcree in turn served to exacerbate the dispute on the Ormeau Road and undermined the attempts at a negotiated settlement. The interconnection between these events, and the wild card introduced by the rioting that followed the release of Lee Clegg, illustrates the problem of trying to deal with each dispute as an isolated and self contained problem.

For the Orangemen each parading dispute was seen as part of a broader threat and challenge to their traditions, their culture and their rights. The mass mobilisation of Orangemen had been widely predicted, and threatened, in the run up to the Twelfth, but most people foresaw the Ormeau Road as the critical location. The stand-off at Drumcree was both a response to the preceding events of the 1995 marching season, but also a reaction to the ongoing local dispute in Portadown, which had been largely quiescent in recent years.

Once the crisis had been dealt with, and the Twelfth had passed for another year, there seems to have been something of a retreat to entrenched positions. There was no public debate of possible long term practical solutions to the problems of parades passing through areas where they were opposed. The negotiations on the Ormeau Road had produced a detailed possible agreement, but this seemed to disappear without trace. It was not used as a possible blueprint for other disputes even though the RUC seemed to regard it as the basis of operational decision making.

Suggestions that a neutral commission should be set up, to mediate on parade disputes, was once again floated, but once again, it was ignored. Unionist politicians, while quick to condemn protests against the parades, seemed unwilling, or unable, to suggest any form of compromise solution. The persistent, low-level violence that continued through the lull in the marching season, indicated that a more positive, pro-active approach was necessary from both sides if the issue was to be resolved.

SECTION 8: LURGAN and DERRY

8.1 Sinn Fein in Lurgan
There are few parades in the two weeks following the Twelfth, and the only reported incident was a minor dispute as a crowd of loyalists protested in the Belmore Street area of Enniskillen when a Saoirse parade was held through the town on 16 July (IN 17-7). When the marching season recommenced in earnest, at the end of July, there was a dispute and confrontation in yet another location: Lurgan. Sinn Fein announced their intention of holding a march and rally in the town on Sunday 30 July, one of a number of similar events calling for all-party peace talks and the disbandment of the RUC. The DUP and the Orange Order both lodged complaints with the RUC; then local loyalists decided that they would hold a counter-rally at a similar time, with the intention of preventing Sinn Fein from marching through the town (BT 27-7).

Announcing a counter rally to prevent nationalist or republican parades and rallies in Ulster is a long standing loyalist tactic, which dates back to the late nineteenth century. In more recent times the practice was adopted to counter civil rights marches in the 1960s. The usual result in such cases has been for both marches or rallies to be banned, but it can have more serious consequences. The announcement of an Apprentice Boys parade over the same route as a planned civil rights rally in Derry in 1968 led the Stormont government to ban both parades. The organisers of the civil rights parades determined to try to hold their march, and the ensuing clashes between police and demonstrators marked the build-up to the Troubles (Bardon 1992, McCann 1980, Purdie 1990).

The loyalist opposition in Lurgan was stirred, not so much by Sinn Fein's demands, but that they should wish to express them in the town centre. David Trimble called the march "provocative" and he described it as a "wholly unprecedented plan by Sinn Fein to march into Lurgan centre ... to cause confrontation". He also justified the opposition by pointing out that Lurgan town centre had only just been rebuilt, following the devastation caused by an IRA bomb three years previously. Although the population of Lurgan is almost equally balanced between Protestants and Catholics, it had witnessed "no serious disturbances since 1972". However, the town has been described as virtually segregated into two distinct parts, which are separated by "an 'invisible line' which divided Catholic from Protestant Lurgan". This line is said to run across Market Street, near to the public toilets (O'Dowd 1993 p 52, SL 30-7, 15-10). It was here that the loyalists planned to hold their rally. They were adamant that the republican marchers would not be allowed go beyond what was described as "the traditional 'back of the church' demarcation line for nationalist marches at the end of Market Street". All previous nationalist parades in the town, had either accepted this limit or they had been re-routed by the RUC (SL 30-7, 15-10).

On the day of the planned parades, the RUC cordoned off the town centre. A crowd of some 1500 loyalist protesters threw a range of missiles as they clashed with the RUC dressed in riot gear. Due to the threat of "serious public disorder" the republican rally was then re-routed by the police. The Sinn Fein supporters paraded from the Francis Street area along Edward Street, but they were stopped by RUC from entering either Church Street or Market Street because of the risk of violence. The marchers held a sit-down protest and rally in front of the police lines, before dispersing peacefully. The loyalist protesters, in turn, were joined by David Trimble and Peter Robinson, deputy leader of the DUP. At their rally, Robinson justified their opposition by claiming that there was no comparison between the events at Drumcree and those at Lurgan, because, he said, there was no such thing as a traditional 'IRA route' into the town. David Trimble declared that their action was a victory for peaceful protest. In contrast Sinn Fein Councillor Brendan Curran said "It is ironic that David Trimble and the DUP's Ian Paisley who, a few weeks ago, were demanding their right as Orangemen to march through a nationalist area are now demanding that nationalists are not allowed to march into a nationalist area" (BT 31-7, IN 31-7, NL 31-7). While Sinn Fein accepted the re-routing and dispersed peacefully, subsequent events have shown that they would not be content with a continuation of their exclusion from the centre of Lurgan. They have made a number of subsequent, but so far, unsuccessful attempts to hold rallies or pickets in the town centre.

8.2 Walking Derry's Walls
In early August attention began to be focused on the forthcoming Apprentice Boys' Relief of Derry celebrations. This anniversary is marked by two parades. In the morning the parent clubs of the Apprentice Boys, which are based in the city of Londonderry, parade in the old city. Until 1969 this parade had completed a circuit of the city walls, but since 1970 the walls have been closed and subsequently the Apprentice Boys had been restricted to parading within, rather than on, the walls. In the afternoon the full membership of the organisation, with numerous bands, parade from the

Waterside, across the Craigavon Bridge and around the Diamond before re-crossing the bridge whence they return to their buses and trains.

In early August, Alistair Simpson, the Governor of the Apprentice Boys, said that an application had been made to walk a full circuit of the walls, which had recently been completely re-opened to the public; he admitted, however, that the RUC had yet to make a decision on whether it would be allowed. He said that their application was not unusual, because they had applied for permission to walk around the walls every year since 1969, and in recent years they had been permitted to walk a small section of them. But he denied that the route could be seen as provocative, and insisted that the Apprentice Boys had never been the cause of violence, even in 1969. This sentiment had earlier been voiced by William Ross MP, who insisted that the march would not infringe on nationalist areas of the city. In response, Sinn Fein claimed that any attempt to walk the area of the walls which overlooked the nationalist Bogside would be provocative and it could easily spark trouble. Their Northern Chairperson, Gerry O hEara, called on the Apprentice Boys to withdraw their application to walk the full circuit of the walls. The SDLP called for all parties to exercise restraint and invited the Apprentice Boys to discuss the matter of the parade with them. This failed to produce a response from the Apprentice Boys. They also refused an invitation from the Mayor of Derry who wanted to discuss both their proposed route and his own suggestion for a three year moratorium on all parades in the city centre (BT 9-8, IN 4-8, 5-8, 8-8, 10-8, NL 15-7).

In Belfast there was opposition to another parade along the Ormeau Road. The Belfast Walker Club wanted to walk from Ballynafeigh to meet their bus which would take them to Londonderry. Sandy Geddis, DUP councillor and president of the club, reiterated their claim that they did not want to cause offence: "We have been walking that route since 1907 and we never had any problems ... We don't even carry a Union Flag". However the residents of the lower Ormeau were still said to be "very angry" over the behaviour of the RUC on the Twelfth of July, and they said they would continue to oppose parades along the road (IN 8-8).

In a surprise move, which received widespread publicity but was also quickly, and widely, condemned, the County Down Amalgamated Committee of the Apprentice Boys threatened to blockade Roman Catholic churches in protest at the continued banning and rerouteing of Orange parades. Martin Smyth and Alistair Simpson both voiced opposition to this proposal, which it was said was nothing more than a suggestion for possible action and had not been adopted by the Apprentice Boys (BT 8-8, IN 9-8, NL 9-8).

In spite of much discussion and speculation, no decisions were made about whether either the Derry parade, or the Ormeau Road parade, would be allowed along their proposed routes until the last minute. The RUC would only confirm that negotiations were continuing in an attempt to ensure that all the Apprentice Boys' parades passed peacefully. Acting Deputy Chief Constable Ronnie Flanagan repeated the RUC's assertion that the police do not give permission for parades to take place, although he agreed that they had power to impose conditions if justified in law. Once again the police appealed for people on both sides of the community to remain calm (IN 11-8).

On the Ormeau Road, the residents announced that they would be holding an all night street party on the eve of the parade, as part of their week long festival, and therefore they expected that there would be more people on the streets than usual when the Apprentice Boys arrived. In Derry a Bogside Residents Group was formed following a public meeting whose members announced that they would oppose the parade in a non-violent manner. On Friday afternoon members of the group occupied a section of the city walls over the Butcher's Gate, and announced that they would stay there to block the parade the following day. Attempts to reach an agreement continued until late into the night. The Apprentice Boys suggested a number of concessions and constraints that they would impose on themselves while walking the walls, but these proved to be insufficient to defuse the protest. The RUC still refused to say if the parades would be allowed to take place or not. It was claimed that this only served to raise the tension in both cities. The uncertainty also increased speculation about what actions supporters on each side might take if they did not get their way.

The issue was confronted first on the Ormeau Road. At about 8 am the police began to remove protesters from Ormeau Bridge to allow the 20 Apprentice Boys and the Lord Carson Memorial Band to parade along the road. As the protesters resisted, officers in riot gear moved in to clear the road. The violence was short lasting but brutal and left 12 RUC and between 11 and 30 civilians injured. One man was wounded by a plastic bullet. Residents from the lower Ormeau blocked the road in the afternoon in protest at the morning's events, but there was no trouble. The Apprentice Boys took a different route back to Ballynafeigh from their outward parade (SL 13-8, SW 13-8, IN 14-8, NL 14-8).

At 9 am on Saturday morning the centre of Derry was full of RUC officers and vehicles. These were concentrated on the approaches to Butcher's Gate where an estimated 200 residents from the Bogside had remained on the walls overnight. Outside the Memorial Hall there was a small number of Apprentice Boys, bandsmen and others. No-one knew what was going to happen. The thirty metres between the nationalist protesters and the Apprentice Boys was occupied by a few police officers and numerous journalists. In an interview, Mark Durcan (SDLP) suggested that a deal, trading the lower Ormeau parade for the circuit of the walls had been offered but not accepted. Around 9.30, Martin McGuinness was interviewed immediately in front of the Memorial Hall. This produced jeers and abuse from the loyalist crowd and a number of women shouted to police nearby "why was he allowed on the walls when we're not".

Shortly after 9.30 the police moved in on the protesters, initially containing them on a small section of the walls above the Butcher's Gate, and then carrying and dragging them from the walls. At the Memorial Hall, cheers went up from the loyalist crowd with the expectation that the parade would be allowed to go ahead. This was the first time that the general air of uncertainty and confusion had changed. At 10 am the barriers were removed and members of the General Committee made their way onto the walls. The first man on to the walls waved his arms in the air and cheered, but most moved quietly into position. The parade set off down towards the Guildhall. The four bands, from Glasgow, Derry, Portadown and Burntollet initially marched to the accompaniment of a single drum beat. Beneath the walls, in front of the youth hostel near Butcher's Gate, the nationalist protesters were surrounded by RUC officers. They stood quietly with their backs to the parade and with their right arms raised giving a clenched fist or a 'V for Victory' sign. The wall was lined with police overlooking the protesters but the marchers ignored the silent demonstration. As the first band reached the part of the walls that were shielded from the Bogside by the buildings of Waterloo Street, they struck up in full tune and each of the three following bands followed the same procedure. As the parade crossed the section of walls overlooking the Guildhall Square they were jeered and barracked by a small number of people below, but otherwise there was no response from beneath the walls. The city centre was very quiet, few shops had bothered to open. After completing the circuit and laying a wreath on the War Memorial, the procession continued to the Cathedral. Many of the Apprentice Boys went into the service, some remained outside as stewards, others went to the initiation of new members in the Memorial Hall, and a few went to a nearby bar.

The main parade began on the Waterside at 12.30 pm. Trouble started late in the afternoon when a band from Portadown arrived in the Diamond. They began to play loudly at a crowd of nationalists nearby and soon missiles were being thrown from both sides. The police moved in to clear the nationalist demonstrators away from the Diamond down Butcher Street and Shipquay Street. After a stand-off the police attempted to force the demonstrators further back out of the walled city. In response the police were attacked by an assortment of missiles and petrol bombs. This began a riot that lasted for several hours and caused tens of thousands of pounds worth of damage (SL 13-8, SW 13-8, IN 14-8, NL 14-8). The trouble was brought under control late in the evening.

The Ancient Order of Hibernians held their annual parade through the city centre on Lady Day, Tuesday 15 August; there was no trouble, nor any protests, but the parade stayed well clear of the loyalist Fountain estate. The following Saturday, nationalists held a parade through the main streets to 'reclaim the city for the community', comparable to the loyalist rally in Castlederg in May. This marked the end to an intensive week of public demonstrations.

The Pat Finucane Centre in Derry published a detailed report on the events of 12 August shortly afterwards. It was extremely critical of the RUC: a) for allowing the parade onto the walls; b) on making the decision so late; and c) in the treatment of the protesters. The report made the following recommendations relating to future parades in the city:

1. The Apprentice Boys should not be allowed to parade on the west wall unless with the agreement of the residents of the Bogside and adjoining areas.
2. The Apprentice Boys should only be allowed to parade in the City centre following satisfactory agreement concerning the stewarding of the parade and the behaviour of the Apprentice Boys. This agreement should be brokered by party leaders on Derry City Council and should involve the General Committee of the Apprentice Boys of Derry, the Chamber of Trade and the Bogside Residents' Group.
3. Political parties, the media and all other organisations involved in the civic life of this city should commit themselves urgently to facilitating good community relations where the different traditions

are respected on the basis of tolerance and equality.
4. Plastic bullets should be banned immediately. The continued use of this lethal weapon is in breach of the ceasefires.
5. As a matter of urgency the crisis in policing must be resolved. No single incident in the past year has demonstrated that urgency clearer than the avoidable events of 12 August 1995.

This report was produced only two weeks after the events in Derry; but, as with all the other recommendations for future action, or possible solutions to the issue of parading disputes, the suggestions were perceived as part of a larger nationalist agenda, and so were largely ignored.

8.3 Protests elsewhere on the Twelfth of August
As well as the violence in Belfast and Derry, there were minor disturbances in several other places later in the day. There were clashes between bandsmen and local people in two predominately nationalist villages, Dunloy and Rasharkin, after bandsmen had returned from the main parade in Derry. In Dunloy the bandsmen were attacked with stones and bottles as they paraded the village. Five people were injured in the resulting scuffles. In Rasharkin a number of bandsmen broke ranks and attacked people on the streets, after a verbal exchange with local youths. At least eight people were assaulted before the Apprentice Boys' marshals were able to restore order. Although this was a relatively minor dispute in Rasharkin, it raised concerns among local people that trouble would flare up again at a band parade that was planned for the village the following week. In the event this parade seems to have passed peacefully. SDLP representative Sean Farren, once again raised the question of why nationalist villages should have to witness Orange parades throughout the summer (Ballymena Chronicle 17-8, BT 19-8, IN 17-8).

In County Fermanagh, there was a dispute in Rosslea, as a crowd of 150 protesters gathered to prevent members of the local Black Preceptory from parading through the town on the same evening. Eventually a compromise was reached and, on the advice of the police, but under protest at the change to their traditional route, the Blackmen agreed to hold a short parade directly to their hall (Fermanagh Herald 16-8). Finally, on the following day, Sunday 13 August, a small group of loyalists attacked a republican Internment Commemoration rally with stones and bottles as it passed the bottom of Divis Street on the way to the City Hall. Republican supporters chased after the loyalists and the RUC eventually came between the two sides. The main body of the parade continued on its way. This seems to have been nothing more than a tit-for-tat response to the protests and rioting in Derry the previous day.

8.4 Summary

Despite the two major confrontations which had been provoked by the issue of parading, and recurrent violence at events across the province, there was still no agreement on a way forward. Each of the three main parties involved - the police, those parading and those protesting - were blamed as contributing to the problem. All sides continued to pass the blame and nobody was prepared to make a serious attempt to confront the issue. There was extensive condemnation of the violence at the parades in both Derry and Belfast, but there was little clarity and no agreement as to what should have been done. The editorials in the three local daily papers illustrate these diverging views. For the *Irish News*, it was clear that the only solution was to keep loyalist parades away from the Ormeau Road and to restrict the Apprentice Boys to a section of the city walls. The paper contrasted the violent police treatment of protesters, and the use of plastic bullets on the Ormeau Road, with the restraint that was shown to loyalist protesters at Lurgan and Larne in July (IN 14-8). The *News Letter* was content to blame the Sinn Fein strategy of creating a "summer of confrontation" for the trouble. It contrasted "the ferocity of the nationalist protests" with the "relatively peaceful parade of Apprentice Boys" (NL 14-8). The *Belfast Telegraph* editorial was headed "Taking Decisions: a new approach is needed". It argued that a better form of decision making was required "so that the police would not be enforcing their own decisions", although it admitted that it would be "too late to take effect this summer". While the paper suggested that a tribunal might be set up to adjudicate on these matters, it also believed that there would be a problem in getting a "balanced tribunal, whose opinions would be respected and obeyed". As an alternative, the Secretary of State could take the decision to ban marches, but this, it admitted, would also be fraught with difficulty. In the meantime it was the duty of parade organisers "to stand back and consider the consequences, for Northern Ireland as a whole, of attempting to march in areas where deep offence is taken ... The right to march has never implied a right to march everywhere" (BT 15-8).

The RUC tactics in Derry, and especially the recourse to plastic bullets, was seen as a major blow to their community relations in the city, just as the rioting and violence was a blow to the image of both the city, and the province as a whole. However, the RUC were in a difficult position with regard to the Apprentice Boys parades. The city of Derry has a particular symbolic significance for the Protestant community and the Relief parades attracts people from all over the north. Once the request to parade the complete circuit of the walls had been made public, there seemed little scope for the Apprentice Boys to accept less, without it appearing as another compromise on their claimed rights. There were rumours of either a Drumcree style stand-off, or a Larne style blockade being imposed if either the parade in Belfast or the main one in Derry were not allowed to go ahead. This possibility seems to have been instrumental in the decision to allow both parades to take place without any conditions being imposed. While there was always a real prospect of violent protests if these parades were allowed to take place, this seems to have been accepted as the lesser evil. Once again, the failure to make a public decision on the issue until the last minute, or to impose a compromise, may have served to inflame the situation. This is not to blame the RUC for the events in Derry; they were left somewhere in the middle ground between two parties who were unwilling to negotiate a compromise.

Although the Twelfth of July and the Relief of Derry are the two major events of the parading calendar, they are far from the end of the marching season. Despite the pessimism of the *Belfast Telegraph* editorial in suggesting that it was too late to change approach to the parades this late in the summer, there were some subtle changes in the way in which the parades were dealt with in the remainder of the marching season.

SECTION 9: THE BLACK PARADES

9.1 Black on the Ormeau
The parades in the second half of August are dominated by those organised by the Royal Black Institution. They hold a number of church and other local parades in advance of the main parade on the last Saturday of the month. Two Black parades were planned to pass along the lower Ormeau Road. On the Monday following the violence at the Apprentice Boys parade, the LOCC announced that they planned to seek a judicial review over the forthcoming Black parade. They said that they would argue before the high court that any loyalist parade on the road would inevitably end in violence and thereby violate the 1987 Public Order (NI) Order. Two days later, the Ballynafeigh Black Preceptory announced that it had decided to re-route both of its planned parades, one to a service at the Presbyterian Assembly Hall on Sunday 20 August, and the other - a feeder parade - to the Last Saturday demonstration in Holywood on Saturday 26 August, away from the lower Ormeau.

The Belfast Grand Master, the Reverend Victor Ryan, said the Preceptory did not want a repeat of the serious violence that had marked the Apprentice Boys parade, or any further confrontation, especially on the way to a Christian service. However, he also said that some of the Preceptory's membership were "very vexed" at the decision and he criticised the lack of a willingness to compromise on the part of the LOCC. Noel Liggett, of Ballynafeigh Orange Lodge, said he supported the suggestion of the Black Preceptory for a wider forum to discuss the parading issue, and he suggested it should include "loyalist orders, local politicians, wider representatives and church leaders". Sir Hugh Annesley, Chief Constable of the RUC, also welcomed the decision as "courageous and truly responsible" and a "very significant contribution to the general stability within the Province". He also restated the police view that it was up to the "people and their political and community representatives to decide how best to reconcile the 'right' to march with the 'right' to protest". The LOCC gave a cautious welcome to the Black Institution's decision, Gerard Rice saying it had been a courageous, if overdue, step. He also defended his right to speak on behalf of the lower Ormeau community and said that a recent petition "showed 85% of people in favour of re-routing these marches". He urged the Orange Order and the Apprentice Boys to follow the example of the Black and cancel any parades that they had planned before the end of the marching season (IN

17-8, 19-8, NL 17-8, 18-8). However Sinn Fein's representative in South Belfast, Sean Hayes, claimed that the Black Preceptory had been forced into re-routing their parades by the RUC, as a result of the decision of the LOCC to seek a judicial review in the high court. He said Sir Patrick Mayhew was not prepared to defend his decision to permit the parade in court and therefore the marchers were given the choice of either re-routing it themselves or having the parade banned (IN 25-8).

9.2 Provincial Protests
In the event there was no trouble on the Ormeau Road at either of the two parade dates. The city and county of Londonderry Black parade took place in the city centre without incident. In contrast with the events two weeks earlier the event passed without incident. Parading on the walls was not part of the Black tradition. City centre shops were open and the atmosphere seemed relatively relaxed. However, there were disturbances at, and following, other Black parades on the Last Saturday, 26 August. In Bellaghy, there were minor scuffles as police broke up a protest by residents who tried to block the route of the local Black Preceptory and its band, as they paraded through the village on their way to the main parade in Derry. The residents had appealed to the Blackmen to cancel their demonstration and thereby "show the courage and respect that their counterparts in Belfast had displayed" and they had also asked the RUC to re-route the parade. Both requests were ignored and instead demonstrators from Bellaghy Residents Group were forcibly removed from the road as the parade was escorted through the village (Mid-Ulster Observer 31-8, IN 26-8, SL 27-8). There was also trouble in Castlederg, which flared up several hours after a County Tyrone Black parade had passed through the town. Disturbances between "rival sectarian gangs" began in the Ferguson Crescent area in the early hours of Sunday morning, and it took the RUC over two hours to restore order. Missiles were thrown by both sides and the police responded with plastic bullets. Twelve police officers and several dozen civilians were injured. Sinn Fein representatives in the town claimed the riots were a follow-on from the earlier parade, but local unionists strongly denied any links between the parade and the rioting. They claimed that all those who had been involved in the parade had gone home long before the trouble began (NL 28-8, Tyrone Constitution 31-8).

In spite of the re-routing of the Black parades away from the Ormeau Road, the Ballynafeigh Orangemen were angry when the RUC announced, on Wednesday 6 September, that they would not be allowed to march along the Ormeau Road to a bicentenary service at St Anne's Cathedral on the following Sunday. Sinn Fein, however, welcomed the RUC decision. Sean Hayes said that they had willingly re-routed their parades away from loyalist areas and he urged the organisers of loyalist parades to show "similar goodwill" and to engage in dialogue with the affected communities. The LOCC were also pleased with the RUC decision but they also said that this was still only a short term resolution to the problem. In contrast Ian Paisley said the police decision only sent another clear message of encouragement to the IRA (IN 7-9, NL 7-9). On the day of the proposed march, members of Ballynafeigh District LOL handed a letter of protest into the local RUC station, and then paraded to the bridge. This time they did not hold a service there but instead drove to the cathedral. A small group of loyalists jeered the Orangemen as they left and continued to protest against the re-routing until the early evening (NL 11-9). A few days later, on Wednesday 13 September, members of a new group calling itself ORDER (Ormeau Residents Demand Equal Rights) held a demonstration outside Ballynafeigh Orange Hall. Led by Ian Paisley Jr., the 200 people marched to the local RUC station and delivered a letter protesting at the continual re-routing of Orange parades. A small group of the protesters then tried to continue the march into the lower Ormeau, but the road was blocked by police Land Rovers and the crowd was persuaded to disperse by Paisley (NL 14-9).

On the evening of 10 Sunday, there had also been more trouble in Dunloy, County Antrim, when Orangemen returning from a bicentenary service in the town's Presbyterian church were attacked by a crowd of 150-200 people who had just returned from a hurling match in Belfast. In the disturbances, a gun was stolen from an RUC officer, but the trouble was soon brought under control. Ian Paisley blamed republicans for the violence, but SDLP Councillor Charlie Kane played the affair down and said that only about half a dozen people were involved. His colleague Sean Farren repeated calls for the establishment of a commission to oversee parading disputes (Ballymena Chronicle 14-9, NL 11-9, NL 12-9).

On Friday 22 September, the evening before the Orange Order's Bicentenary Rally in Loughgall, County Armagh, there were minor disturbances at a band parade in Downpatrick. On the Wednesday before the planned parade, the RUC re-routed it away from Church Street and the town centre "to prevent serious public disorder or serious damage to property", just as they had in previous years. The parade organisers, protested against the re-routing, and, throughout the two hours of the parade, each of the 19 bands marched up to the barriers across the end of Church Street and played party tunes directly at the police. The music was greeted with volleys of assorted missiles and fire-crackers which were thrown at the police by members of the watching crowd. The event rarely looked like getting out of control, and although one man was arrested and two policemen were slightly injured, the evening ended quietly after the bands had finished parading (IN 21-9).

In early October Sinn Fein announced that once again it would attempt to hold a rally in the centre of Lurgan, this time on Sunday the 8th. The DUP immediately announced that it would hold a counter demonstration against Sinn Fein at the same time which would be addressed by Ian Paisley. As a result of the DUP action, the RUC imposed conditions on both parties, restraining them from entering the town centre (NL 6-10, SL 8-10). Extra RUC were drafted into Lurgan to control the rival republican and loyalist gatherings. The town centre, between the two police lines, was deserted and both demonstrations passed peacefully (IN 9-10, NL 9-10). The following Saturday, two people were arrested when a crowd of about 100 republican supporters tried to complete the parade route which had been banned the previous week and walked in single file around the island at the 'nationalist' end of the main street. The police seemed surprised at first but eventually broke up the demonstration. A police spokesperson said "we simply moved them out of the centre where they are not welcomed by the vast majority of decent respectable people, nationalist and loyalist" and he accused Sinn Fein of "continuing to provoke confrontation" in the town. Sinn Fein responded by accusing the RUC of using "brutal" tactics. Another minor clash occurred two weeks later, when Sinn Fein once again tried to hold a peaceful demonstration in the town centre and the RUC insisted on moving them on, once again making a number of arrests (SW 15-10, IN 30-10).

9.3 The season draws to a close
The final scenes of a long marching season were again largely played out in Belfast in late October. On 13 October loyalists held a massive rally in Belfast city centre to mark the anniversary of the Combined Loyalist Military Command ceasefire. Four parades converged from different areas of the city but organisers made it clear well in advance that they did not plan to go anywhere near the lower Ormeau. The scale of support took

most people by surprise but the event was well stewarded and caused no trouble (BT 14-10, IN 3-10, 14-10). But objections continued at other parades. The republican prisoners support group, Saoirse, planned to hold a parade from the Markets to the lower Ormeau to unveil a mural on Sunday 22 October. However, residents and members of ACORD from Donegall Pass claimed that the march was "deliberately provocative". In response to the protest the RUC said the proposed route was unacceptable and suggested that the Saoirse parade walk along the Lagan towpath as an alternative. A Saoirse spokesperson said the idea of using the towpath was ridiculous, and announced that they would re-route their parade to avoid confrontation. In the end the parade began from McClure Street beside the railway bridge, rather than in the Markets, and the crowd walked peacefully to the mural at Dromara Street (IN 21-10, 23-10, NL 20-10). On the same day a republican parade was held in north Belfast to mark the second anniversary of the death of IRA volunteer Thomas Begley. This created widespread anger on the Shankill Road as Begley had died planting the bomb that destroyed Frizzell's fish shop and killed nine other people. The parade, from the Antrim Road to the Ardoyne, was organised by the Carrick Hill Flute Band, of which Thomas Begley was once a member. As a result of the reaction among loyalists in west Belfast, the Tanaiste, Dick Spring, was forced to cancel a meeting with members of the Progressive Unionist Party which they had planned to hold on the Shankill Road and which was instead relocated to the Europa Hotel (IN 23-10, NL 24-10). The final Orange parade planned for the Ormeau Road, on Sunday October 29, was banned by the RUC on 26 Thursday, after members of the LOCC had again announced that they would seek permission to hold a judicial review in a bid to stop the Reformation Day parade to St Anne's Cathedral. In response to the re-routing, it was reported that the Ballynafeigh Orangemen had put out an unofficial appeal for mass support. According to a senior figure in the Orange Order: "They want a Drumcree style demonstration of support". However only about 100 people turned up for the protest service and rally at the Ormeau Bridge. Although the police maintained a large presence in blocking the bridge there was no counter demonstration on the other side (IN 26-10, 27-10, NL 28-10, 30-10, SL 29-10).

9.4 Summary
There were no major disputes over parades after the rioting in Derry in August, but, ominously, minor disputes occurred in a wider range of

locations than previously. In particular, the persistent clashes in Castlederg and Lurgan, and to a less extent the disputes in Bellaghy, Dunloy and Rasharkin may suggest a broadening of the dispute in the future. It is therefore interesting to note the change in tactics on the Ormeau Road by all three principal parties. The LOCC decided to take legal action over the heads of the police. They appealed directly to the Northern Ireland Office and demanded that the parades be banned in advance. They argued that recent events meant that any parade along the road would produce "serious public disorder". However, they were never able to test their case before the high court because of the actions of the Black Preceptory and the police. In the first instance, the Black Preceptory announced that they were voluntarily re-routing their two parades. They claimed that as a Christian organisation, they had no wish to provoke violence. In response, Sinn Fein claimed that pressure had been brought to bear by the RUC, that the Black had the choice of voluntarily re-routing, or being banned. There has been no confirmation of this. The Orange Order offered no such concessions with regard to their final two parades, but in both cases the RUC ordered a compulsory re-routing away from the lower Ormeau. A relatively low key attempt to attract outside support for their cause fell on deaf ears, and few people outside of the local lodge turned up on the Ormeau Road. It has been claimed that the RUC decision to ban the parade some days in advance was a response to the appeal for a judicial review lodged by the LOCC. However, the police decision also follows the logic that they were acting as if the agreement between the Orangemen and the LOCC, agreed in July, was still in place. This had stated that there would be no Orange parades through the lower Ormeau after the Twelfth of July. At the same time it was likely that the violent clashes at the two parades which were pushed through the lower Ormeau would be repeated if any other parades were allowed. These two parades, therefore, became the standard by which to judge the opposition to loyalist parades. Whatever the reason behind the changed response, the final re-routed parades passed off peacefully. The LOCC did not need to mobilise large numbers of supporters on the streets and most members of the Ballynafeigh Protestant community were not significantly angered to protest.

SECTION 10: OVERVIEW OF THE DISPUTED PARADES

From figures provided by the RUC Central Statistics Unit, the RUC in 1995 recorded 22 parades at which conditions were applied, and 13 at which there was disorder. However, no figures are available sub-dividing parades by organisation. As such, this overview of disputed parades has been constructed by collating press reports. During the 1995 marching season there was a total of 41 parades which generated some form of public protest or some form of violent incident. The police may, however, have imposed conditions on other parades. The disputed parades are listed in Table 10.1. Thirteen of the disputes were at republican parades and 28 at loyalist parades. The loyalist parades include:

- 15 organised by the Orange Order,
- 5 organised by the Apprentice Boys of Derry,
- 5 organised by the Royal Black Institution,
- 3 Band Parades.

The thirteen republican parades include 5 organised by Saoirse, and 8 others; of these 6 were commemorations - four established events (traditional) and two held for the first time in 1995. The other two parades were political rallies.

Although the disputes were spread across the whole of the marching season, nearly half (19/41) occurred in the first half of July and the second half of August. The first half of the marching season ended in a climax on the Twelfth of July. The second half began with a flurry of disputes on 12 August but then tailed off into a number of small and relatively peaceful disputed parades.

10.1 Typology of Disputed Parades
Using the typology outlined earlier, the disputed loyalist parades include:

Feeder Parades	10
Church Parades	8
Band Parades	3
Mini-12th	3
Main Parades	2
Special Parades	2

The main commemorative parades were only the locus of trouble in the case of the Relief of Derry parade, the other incident listed was the rioting that followed the RBI Last Saturday parade in Castlederg, the main parade itself had passed peacefully. However, over 25% of the disputed parades (11/41) occurred on three main anniversary days: three disputes on the Twelfth, five on the anniversary of the Relief of Derry, and three on the Last Saturday. Nine of these parades involved small feeder parades, which were being held in places well away from the location of the main event. Another five disputed parades were held in the run-up to the Twelfth, three mini-Twelfth parades and two church parades. Given that the pre-Twelfth period seems to be an increasingly popular period for local mini-Twelfth type of parades, the numbers of disputes in this period may well increase in future years. The main Twelfth parades usually pass peacefully, with any opposition most commonly expressed by ignoring, or avoiding, the event rather than actually opposing the parades. Instead, it is the overall scale of the celebrations that seems to provoke opposition and, in particular, it is the widespread insistence on holding local parades prior to departing for the major events that creates resentment. Although church parades appear prominently on the list, six of the eight disputed parades were along the Ormeau Road, which were seen as intrusive local parades, and another was the Drumcree Church parade. Church parades usually attract little attention, except in particular places, as they are relatively quiet and attract few supporters. But as a part of the more extensive marching season they increase the visibility of Orange parades.

Band parades do not provoke much opposition either. Despite large numbers of band parades throughout the marching season there were protests at only three events. This is probably because most band parades are held in areas that are clearly defined as Protestant, and rarely have the freedom, that is given to parades organised by the loyal order, to parade where they will. In the majority of cases the organisers of band parades steer clear of interface areas. It was perhaps notable that, when supporters of the loyalist paramilitary groups organised a rally in Belfast city centre to mark the first anniversary of the loyalist ceasefire on 13 October, they made the point, on numerous occasions in the run up to the event, that they would avoid parading anywhere near the Ormeau Road.

Where there was opposition to band parades, it occurred at those few that are held in towns with a large nationalist population. There have been protests at loyalist parades through the largely nationalist village of Pomeroy on several occasions in recent years. At Castlederg the protests seem to have been primarily a response to the recent re-routing of a repub-

Table 10.1: Parade Re-routings, Disputes & Violence in 1995

Date	Location	Organisation	Type	
April				
Mon 17	Ormeau Road	Apprentice Boys	Feeder	(C)
Sun 23	Ormeau Road	Orange Order	Church	(C)
Sun 30	Castlederg	Saoirse	Protest	(C)
May				
Thurs 4	Ormeau Road	Orange Order	VE Day	(C)
	Short Strand	Orange Order	VE Day	(A)
Sat 6	Castlederg	Band Parade		(T)
Sun 7	Ormeau Road	Republican	H-S Comm	(V)
	Suffolk	Republican	H-S Comm	(C)
Sat 13	Pomeroy	Band Parade		(P)
Sat 28	Castlederg	Republican		(P)
June				
Sun 18	Ormeau Road	Orange Order	Church	(C)
Sat 24	Springfield Rd	Orange Order	Mini-12th	(T)
July				
Sun 2	Ormeau Road	Orange Order	Church	(C)
Wed 5	Ormeau Road	Orange Order	Mini-12th	(V)
	Bellaghy	Orange Order	Mini-12th	(P)
Sun 9	Portadown	Orange Order	Church	(T)
Wed 12	Ormeau Road	Orange Order	Feeder	(T)
	Portadown	Orange Order	Feeder	(C)
	Short Strand	Orange Order	Feeder	(A)
Sun 16	Enniskillen	Saoirse		(P)
Sun 30	Lurgan	Saoirse		(C)
August				
Sat 12	Derry	Apprentice Boys	Main	(T)
	Ormeau Road	Apprentice Boys	Feeder	(T)
	Dunloy	Apprentice Boys	Feeder	(T)
	Rasharkin	Apprentice Boys	Feeder	(T)
	Rosslea	RBI	Feeder	(V)
Sun 13	Suffolk	Republican	Internment	(V)
	Falls Road	Republican	Internment	(T)
Sun 20	Ormeau Road	RBI	Church	(V)
Sat 26	Ormeau Road	RBI	Feeder	(V)
	Bellaghy	RBI	Feeder	(P)
	Castlederg	RBI	Main	(A)
September				
Sun 3	Pomeroy	Republican	Ceasefire	(C)
Sun 10	Ormeau Road	Orange Order	Church	(C)
	Dunloy	Orange Order	Church	(T)
	Bessbrook	Republican	Protest	(C)
Fri 22	Downpatrick	Band Parade		(C)
October				
Sun 8	Lurgan	Saoirse		(C)
Sun 22	Ormeau Road	Saoirse		(V)
	North Belfast	Republican	Comm	(P)
Sun 29	Ormeau Road	Orange Order	Church	(C)

V = Voluntary Re-routing, C = Compulsory Re-routing, P = Protest,
T = Trouble during the parade, A = Trouble after parade.

lican parade, while the Downpatrick band parade has been described as a "traditional re-routing", where the dispute is between the bands and the police. Band parades can rarely evoke the weight of tradition needed to justify parading through nationalist areas.

Recently it was reported that a senior member of the Orange Order was blaming the bands for causing much of the trouble at Orange parades (BT 13-1-96). However, it is difficult to sustain this argument when reviewing the events of last year. Although the bands were always prominent, and both highly visible and extremely audible, they were not responsible for the organisation of the majority of the disputed parades, nor for the stewarding of the parades, although bands are always responsible for the discipline of their own members. One band appears to have been instrumental in provoking trouble in Derry, and bands were named as being involved in disturbances at six other events. But, as we have been told by many bandsmen in their defence, because the bandsmen are so visible at such occasions they are easy targets to blame. This is not to suggest that all bandsmen are angels; they will often be found in the thick of things if trouble arises, and their music can readily rouse sectarian passions. But the bands do not organise most of the parades which are disputed; they always have to be invited by members of a loyal order onto these parades. Before parading with the loyal orders, each band has to sign a contract which sets out the expected standards of behaviour, deportment and displays, and the loyal orders have the authority to ban any bands (and their own members) who cause problems from taking part in future parades. If it is felt that Bands have caused problems it is clearly the responsibility of the parade organisers to deal with the issue in the first instance. It could therefore be argued that there should be greater insistence that the loyal orders take fuller responsibility for all aspects of the parades that they organise.

10.2 Compulsory and Voluntary Re-routing
If we consider the question of voluntary and compulsory re-routing, we can see that only the Royal Black Institution, among the loyal orders, agreed voluntarily to re-route any of their parades. The only Orange parades that have been classed as voluntarily re-routed were the Ballynafeigh mini-Twelfth and the Garvaghy Road feeder parade on the Twelfth. In the first case the re-routing was virtually imposed after the displays at the 1992 mini-Twelfth, and it was widely claimed that the re-

routing of the Portadown parade was imposed as part of the solution to the stand-off at Drumcree. Voluntary re-routing in these cases is something of a misnomer as it only seems to occur when the organisation concerned is faced with the alternative of a police ban on the parade.

The continuation of disputes throughout the summer brought no real hint of compromise. Even in the cases where the Black Preceptories re-routed their own parades, on the Ormeau and in Rosslea, there appeared to be little choice, it was either that or have the parade banned. Voluntary re-routing was not publicly offered as a gesture of compromise, it was always grudgingly done and therefore it lost much of its power. Furthermore, in both cases where the Black re-routed their parade, there were expressions of discontent from within the membership, which undermined the gesture still more. None of these cases can be seen as an attempt to claim the moral high ground.

Table 10.2. The type of Parade in dispute, and those which were re-routed

	Disputes	Church	Feeder	Mini	Main
Orange Order	15 (1V,7C)	7 (5C)	5 (2C)	4 (1V)	-
ABOD	5 (1C)	-	4 (1C)	-	1
RBI	5 (3V)	1 (1V)	3 (1V)	-	1 (1V)
Republican	13 (3V,6C)	-	-	-	-

V = Voluntarily Re-routing, C = Compulsory Re-routing.

The republican groups appeared to be more willing to re-route their own parades. However, two of the voluntary re-routings were at parades planned for the Ormeau Road. Once loyalist residents from the Donegall Pass area objected to the parade passing across the bottom of their road, the organisers were left with little choice. The other case was at Suffolk, where an earlier parade had been compulsorily re-routed, when the second parade generated protests it was speedily re-routed. In Castlederg republicans managed to overcome initial police objections to their parading into the town centre but in Lurgan the campaign to be allowed to parade into the town centre goes on.

10.3 Locating the Disputes

The parading disputes were spread over the length and breadth of Northern Ireland, although half of the disputes were in Belfast and one in three was focused on the Ormeau Road.

BELFAST	21	
Ormeau Road	14	(8 OO, 2 AB, 2 RBI, 2 Rep)
Short Strand	2	(2 OO)
Suffolk	2	(2 Rep)
Other	3	(1 OO, 2 Rep)
CASTLEDERG	4	(1 Band, 1 RBI, 2 Rep)
BELLAGHY	2	(1 OO, 1 RBI)
DUNLOY	2	(1 OO, 1 AB)
LURGAN	2	(2 Rep)
POMEROY	2	(1 Band, 1 Rep)
PORTADOWN	2	(2 OO)
BESSBROOK	1	(1 Rep)
DERRY	1	(AB)
DOWNPATRICK	1	(Band)
ENNISKILLEN	1	(Rep)
RASHARKIN	1	(AB)
ROSSLEA	1	(RBI)

There are two main points involved in understanding and (perhaps) predicting the geography of the disputes. One factor is the widely acknowledged division of much of Northern Ireland into Protestant and Catholic areas. The other major factor in the present dispute, is the loyalist insistence on the primacy of their "traditional" rights to walk along their "traditional" routes without acknowledging any recognition of demographic change. Most of the above disputes have been provoked by members of one community wanting to parade through an area that is identified by members of the other community as belonging to them.

Historically, the state of Northern Ireland, particularly under the Stormont government, was considered to be Protestant. The Catholic community had few opportunities to express their identity through holding public parades, outside of specifically acknowledged Catholic areas. In contrast the loyal orders felt they had the right to parade wherever they wished, and this right was regularly exercised, although it may well have been contested: a recurrent dispute ensued in Dungiven in the 1950s and 1960s over the demands of Orangemen to parade through the town. A town with a large Catholic majority was not regarded as off limits for a Protestant parade, while a small Protestant community could successfully oppose a Catholic parade. Nevertheless, there were still particular areas where loyalists never demanded the right to march.

A traditional parade could therefore become established in spite of the opposition of the local population. This appears to be the source of the disputes over Orange parades in places like Bellaghy and Pomeroy. In both cases those opposing the loyalist parades cite the 80% or 90% nationalist population, while the loyal orders invoke their traditional rights. In towns like Lurgan and Castlederg, respective sectarian areas appear to be widely acknowledged, and the disputes are over whether republican groups should have the same access to the town centre as loyalist groups have. In both cases the republican military campaign is invoked to prohibit access, an argument equivalent to the Unionist quarantining of Sinn Fein from political talks.

In other areas it has been demographic changes that have generated opposition to traditional parades. The residents of the Garvaghy Road and the lower Ormeau Road would acknowledge that Orangemen have paraded along both roads for many years. They would also argue that the situation has changed dramatically in recent years. In the case of the Garvaghy Road, what was until recently a rural area has now become incorporated into the urban sprawl of Portadown. Previously unoccupied fields have become a nationalist housing estate. In the case of the Ormeau Road, an area that was until recently a mixed area, with a sizeable Protestant population, is now an almost totally nationalist area. Many other examples of similar changes can be found across Northern Ireland. Boal (1995) has noted how the Troubles have created differing responses from the two communities in Belfast. Working class Protestants have tended to move away from the inner-city areas and out to the suburbs of Newtownabbey, Lisburn and North Down, while the Catholic community has consolidated its position within the inner-city. These types of changes, which have reinforced an already existing mosaic-like pattern of distinct segregated communities, are a significant factor in many of the disputes over parades.

Besides the more readily explained logic of the disputes one must also be aware of the symbolic significance of particular places as this helps to underpin both the claims of tradition and the resentment of the parades. Tradition itself can contribute to symbolic power and Portadown is a town with a special symbolic significance for Orangeism. The Order was founded in north Armagh and it has long been rooted in Portadown. A recent book on the subject named the town 'The Orange Citadel'. Within this local tradition the parade route from Drumcree has been given particular significance because of the length of time Orangemen have been visiting the church for a service in early July. Regardless of whether the parade has been held annually since the early 19th century, and regardless of numerous probable variations in the route over the years, it has a powerful resonance among local Orangemen.

Likewise in Derry, the symbolic power that the siege has on the Ulster Protestant thinking is well known. For that reason the city is probably the single most important place in the North. Coming to Derry for the Relief celebrations has been likened to a pilgrimage in which walking the walls is the central act of homage, which reconnects the present day Apprentice Boys with the defenders of 1689. For many the Relief parade is the most important event in the commemorative calendar. But for the residents in the Bogside the parade provokes an opposite response: allowing the Apprentice Boys to walk the walls recalls the annual taunts from those on the walls and all the gerrymandered injustices of Derry under Stormont, a part of the city's past that they thought had been left behind. The contrasting right to parade in Derry was the spark that ignited the Troubles in 1968-69.

The symbolic power of the Ormeau Road is of more recent origin, for in this case the spark was the murder of local people in Sean Graham's bookmakers in 1992 and the response by Orangemen on the mini-Twelfth parade. The rationale of "it only takes 5 minutes to pass by" does not cut much ice among the residents. But the Orangemen also respond by asking why that event is remembered and not others where they have suffered; they tell of killings and explosions and of having grown up in the area and having been forced to move in the early years of the Troubles. In each of these three cases it is the less tangible symbolic importance that perpetuates the dispute rather than the hard logic of 'alternative routes' or 'no real disruption'.

This is also what makes the general issue so intractable. For those not immediately involved it is easy to find compromises and solution, but for those intimately involved on either side the local dispute resonates with larger issues. Each parade which is challenged is a symbolic threat to

Protestant security and the unionist position, while each parade which passes through a nationalist area is a restatement of the dominance of the Protestant community and the inferiority of nationalist rights.

PART 3

SECTION 11: ATTITUDES TO AND PERCEPTIONS OF PARADES

The previous sections have reviewed the organisations involved in loyalist parades and the range of parades in which they take part, suggesting some of the historical dimensions that might explain why there are so many loyalist parades compared with republican parades and providing a detailed examination of the disputed events in 1995. This section goes on to analyse the different perceptions that inform the groups involved in the disputes and examines the role of two other institutions that play a role in the dynamics of the conflict - the police and the media.

Many of the views put forward in this section are public knowledge; in addition, a range of individuals and groups connected with the parade disputes has been interviewed - the loyal institutions, resident groups, mediators and police. Some of the results of those interviews inform what follows. Whilst some of the material can be talked about in a general sense, this section tries to draw out some of the elements specific to particular areas which impinge upon the way parades in those areas are understood. Before doing this, however, it is as well to draw together some of the points already covered to try to analyse why parades appear so important in the everyday politics of Northern Ireland.

11.1 The Importance of parades - and why so many?
In a previous study from the Centre for the Study of Conflict, suggestions were made to explain why ritual occasions, such as parades, are seen by participants and many non-participants as being so important. In particular, it was argued that the formalised and routinised nature of such events and their repetitiveness over time gives the impression of social continuity - of tradition (Bryan, Fraser & Dunn 1995:9-13). Part One of this study offers a more detailed analysis of the type of occasions on which parades take place, and suggests some of the differences between localities. Parades attempt to assert a general identity but also reassert a specific local identity. For instance, not all mini-Twelfths are understood in the same way. In some areas the 'mini-Twelfth' is specifically held on 1 July to commemorate the Battle of the Somme. This is the case in the long-standing parades in east Belfast and Sandy Row. In other areas they are simply a way of gearing up for the oncoming Twelfth: Portadown District

only established their mini-Twelfth in 1990; it is held in June and has a different, locally related, theme each year. Parades reflect identities and interests at a number of levels, not just at a more general political level.

It is interesting that in *The Order on Parade*, published recently by the Grand Orange Lodge of Ireland Education Committee, the 'sense of tradition' is taken up as one of the central reasons for parading. The authors describe the 'sense of linking with past generations' and the confidence and pride in taking part in a ritual parade' (Montgomery & Whitten 1995:7). The impression given by this argument is one of the Protestant community expressing unity and continuity over time. However, the authors fail to take account of the rapid increase in both the number and the range of parades over recent years (see Part One). As ritual events, parades may give the impression of a lack of change, and many participants understand them as 'traditional', and therefore depoliticised; but they are clearly part of the present political situation. The perception of 'tradition' effectively masks the changes that are taking place. Indeed, it could be argued that the insecurity produced by the turmoil in Northern Ireland over the previous thirty years is one of the reasons that there has been an increase in the assertion of 'tradition'. It is precisely at times of change that communities require certain identifications with a past to be perceived as more secure. Ironically then the assertion of 'tradition' is made in response to broader forces of political change.

The political changes that have taken place are reflected in the number and form of parades. From the mid-1960s the Unionist block has come under considerable political pressure. Since that time a number of political groups have come into existence, some of whom have just as quickly left the scene (see Bruce 1986, 1992). Whilst the Ulster Unionist Party still has the largest electoral support, the DUP is now a significant feature of Northern Ireland politics and Ian Paisley has been the dominant personality within Unionism, as well as the most durable. The Progressive Unionist Party and Ulster Democratic Party may as yet lack a democratic mandate, but they nevertheless carry overt support in a number of areas and are seen as a possible last line of defence by some. These changes in Unionist politics have had consequences for the loyal orders and for parading. At present, the Orange Institution retains its institutional link to the Ulster Unionist Party. The head of the Orange and Black Institutions are high profile members of the Ulster Unionist Party and Westminster MPs. Yet many in the Orange Institution support other political parties and have become increasingly disenchanted with the leadership offered by the Grand Orange Lodge. In terms of parading this has revealed itself in two ways. Firstly, it has weakened the ability of senior members of the Institution to influence local political situations. We have already pointed out that a local identity and local independence are powerfully present within the Orange Institution, and, if the association of senior members with the Ulster Unionist Party is added, one can begin to understand the importance placed on local events and decision-making. Details of the events of 1995, discussed in Part Two, provide ample evidence of this. Those members of the Orange Institution from outside the Portadown area who were involved in negotiations were always aware of the limitations of their position as outsiders. Despite this, the dominant figure at Drumcree both in terms of media representation and crowd control was Ian Paisley who is neither in the Orange Institution nor from Portadown. Paisley was able to legitimise his presence, on the platform and at the negotiations, in terms of his position as an MEP for Northern Ireland, but the reality is that he carried significant support amongst those in the field. As one of those interviewed put it - 'Paisley represented the crowd'. In other words, those that take part in parades, Orangemen, bandsmen, and spectators are less politically unified than the parade might appear to suggest. This is revealed both in their perceptions of the parades (discussed below) and in the diverse actions and reactions during parading disputes. The disparate nature of Orangeism increases the importance of local parades in relation to the major commemorative parades. It therefore misses the point to suggest to an Orangeman that their parade is just one of 2,500 other 'Orange' parades, because it is *their* parade which is politically and socially significant for them.

The second significant effect of the greater political diversity within unionism has to do with the number and range of parades. The variety of institutions involved in parades reflect that political diversity to some extent. New factions within unionism need to legitimate themselves by drawing upon the past - using names and symbols that indicate a loyalist heritage - and by going out on parade. This is most obviously true in the popularity of blood and thunder bands, discussed in Section 2, and the consequent development of competitive and commemorative band parades, discussed in Section 3. The bands are the common link between all types of parade. Nevertheless, there are very real tensions between the bands and the loyal orders, particularly the Orange Institution. Editions of the UDA and UVF magazines that are produced around the July period are often critical of senior Orangemen, yet strident in the defence of the right to march. Since the 1970s the Orange Institution has distanced itself from paramilitary groups and has attempted to control, albeit not always successfully, both the behaviour of bands and the appearance of paramilitary insignia on the main commemorative parades. Many local lodges are much more at ease with the roles the bands attempt to play in parades than are senior Orangemen. Indeed, the lack of success in imposing controls on local events, indicates, yet again the lack of power in the hierarchy of Orange Institution. Elements of the Orange tradition appear in paramilitary regalia, and references to paramilitary groups and figures can be found on some flags and banners carried on parades. On the other hand, there are examples where there have been clear divisions between the Orange Institution and the bands. In Downpatrick, the annual band parade has been consistently re-routed from the centre of the town, while events organised by the Orange and Black Institutions continue to go through the town. The local police differentiate between a band parade and an Orange parade, a situation which the local District Orange Lodge has been happy to accept.

There are also differences between the loyal orders despite the significant overlap in membership. The more conservative Black Institution has a high number of elderly members and appears to be more likely to avoid controversy by re-routing parades than the Orange and the Apprentice Boys. The Black is seen by members as the most religious of the orders and it is less willing to accept the more overtly political symbols in its parades. On the other hand, the Apprentice Boys are generally more independent in their political position, with their politics perhaps leaning towards that of the DUP. Unlike the Orange Institution they have no formal links with the UUP, and therefore may be a little more acceptable to supporters of the DUP. Ian Paisley is at present a member of the Apprentice Boys, although even that relationship has not been without its problems. The Apprentice Boys do not appear to be as strict with regard to the type of flags flown at their parades, to the extent that in the last few years Ulster Independence flags have been carried by some clubs.

Ironically, it is the very diffuseness of power within loyalism that has led to the plethora of different types of parades that now take place. Different sections draw upon parading for their own legitimacy and as a sign of their greater loyalty. To people outside the bands and the loyal orders, each parade is just one more 'Orange march', but to those taking part each parade holds particular personal localised political significance. To many people outside the bands and loyal orders it feels like the parades are a conspiracy to rule the streets of Northern Ireland each summer, whereas to those taking part each particular parade expresses its own variant of an increasingly disparate loyalism. The greater number of parades is not a reflection of the strength and unity of the unionist cause, rather it is an indication of just the opposite.

Taking into account the wide range of parades that exist, it is worth examining in more detail the ways in which the different parties involved in the disputes perceive what is taking place. Political differences between groups are of course quite real: but some of those misunderstandings stem from different perceptions of what parades mean. Increasing understanding may not cure the problem, but it might offer insights into the feeling involved, and it may also provide some reasons why mediation of disputes has been so difficult.

11.2 Why are loyalist parades opposed?
In the past year 'residents groups' have appeared in opposition to parades in a number of areas. Those organising parades have been quick to categorise these groups as Sinn Féin-inspired organisations, there to attack Protestant culture. Clearly republican activists feel strongly over the issue and are involved in opposition. But the depth of resentment over parades spreads far wider than the republican movement, and includes at least a proportion of those from the Protestant community. Resentment also goes much further back than the forming of residents groups. This resentment is not simply the result of recent short term political agitation, but is rooted in the power structures which Orangeism continues to symbolise to many in the nationalist community. One member of a residents group explained the resentment to Orange parades simply: 'it is about oppression, continued oppression'.

The perception that the Orange Institution is an 'instrument of oppression' is drawn firstly from the understanding that the commemoration of the Battle of the Boyne is 'triumphalist' - the commemoration of a victory of Protestants over Roman Catholics - and secondly from the actual experiences of many Catholics since Northern Ireland was established. There is much about a parade that can be perceived as triumphalist. The banners carry images of battles and individuals deemed central to the Protestant cause. Not only is King William's sword invariably aloft, but the ranks of the individuals on parade are guarded by weapons such as swords and pikes, albeit that these weapons are symbolic and ceremonial. Many of the tunes played by the bands commemorate victories over Catholics - at Derry, at the Boyne, at the Diamond and at Dolly's Brae. The chant by supporters of 'we're up to our necks in fenian blood, surrender or you'll die' is hardly likely to make a watching Catholic feel at ease. For many Catholics there is little that is religious about the Orange Institution, it celebrates and represents political victories - it is triumphalist.

The Orange Institution, however, is seen as more than simply symbolising triumphalism. It was, and to a certain extent is, part of the Northern Ireland state, from which many Catholics feel alienated. The connections between the Orange Institution and Stormont governments are well documented and undeniable (Harbinson 1973, Bew, Gibbon & Patterson 1995). Fionnuala O Connor has described some of these recollections in her valuable work *In Search of a State: Catholics in Northern Ireland*: 'The memories are of the noise and bluster of the Twelfth, police guarding Orangemen who drum their way past Catholic homes and churches ... ' (O'Connor 1993:152)

In the early 1970s residents of the lower Ormeau Road had their roads blocked by high screens and army jeeps on the Twelfth of July, and in some places these tactics are still used. Indeed, one year residents were bussed down to Newcastle in County Down to avoid the Twelfth, only to find another Orange parade taking place there! In 1972 residents of Obins Street in Portadown saw 50 UDA men line the route of an Orange parade apparently with a view to protecting it. The general feeling was that, whatever Orangemen would get up to the police would protect the parade route.

Since the demise of Stormont, Orange parades have still been able to take place relatively unhindered and they seem to grow in number year by year. They are perceived as an attempt to reassert territorial dominance. Catholic and Protestant areas have become highly segregated and demarcated and, whilst Orangemen have continued to march over streets in nationalist areas, nationalists have been unable to march in their own town centres. These feeling are particularly acute in Portadown and Lurgan where a large number of loyalist parades take place, whilst no nationalist parades are allowed into the town centre. At a meeting late in 1995 two members of the Garvaghy Road Residents Group in Portadown summarised the situation:

Nationalists in Portadown live in one corner ... Parades go on in Portadown for two, if not three, months - every Saturday morning

I'm woken up to the sound of Orange bands banging their drums in the town, because we can hear everything, its not a big town, we can here everything from where we are. Everyone will tell you it's a terror to go, if you're going shopping at the weekends or even sometimes during the week, because you're stopped at a parade and there's absolutely nothing you can do. Over the streets in Portadown there are 6 arches representing 'No surrender', 'Victory' and statues of King Billy, and while they're going up everyone has to wait and put up with them and the place is covered with flags.

In Portadown unionists outnumber nationalists by roughly a 4:1 majority, with the nationalist community living in one small corner of the town consisting mainly of the Garvaghy Road and Obins Street. Each July the whole town, especially the town centre, becomes saturated with red, white and blue bunting, Union Jacks and images of King Billy. The sense of tension is very high during this period. Many weekly shopping trips to the town centre are abruptly ended as the news spreads of yet another loyalist band parade and panic sets in until you reach the safe haven of home ... Many teenagers are afraid to go shopping in the evenings after school, afraid their religion might be recognised through their school uniforms.

The number of parades that take place appears to many nationalists to be threatening and a constant irritation. All the organisations seem the same to them - Orange, Black, Apprentice Boys - the same people with the same bands. The reasons for parades appear to be just another excuse to impose themselves in areas where they are not wanted; it is argued that it is not necessary to hold a parade to go to church. On the lower Ormeau they are particularly baffled as to why members of the loyal orders need to parade into the city centre to get onto a bus to travel to a venue miles away. Streets are blocked by police so that people cannot go shopping. In short, in areas where communities are so clearly bounded, why is there a need for a group to parade where it is not wanted? It appears to be little more than 'coat trailing'.

A further aspect of the resentment felt towards 'Orange parades' is the massive policing that accompanies them. The police are seen to be protecting the parades and hemming residents in. For many people who view the police with suspicion anyway, the police almost appear to be part of the parade, as they lead the Orangemen down the road. The sensitivities of those in the area are perceived to be largely ignored and suspicions often remain that the police are doing the bidding of those in the parade. Because of the volatile nature of the disputed parades the scale of the police operations appears to residents as oppressive. In Bellaghy hundreds of police enter the town to protect the parades. On the Twelfth of July the area of the lower Ormeau was effectively sealed off to force the parade through. A further operation for the Apprentice Boys parade in August led to some ugly scenes as police discipline appeared to break down. Similarly, on the Garvaghy Road, the intensive policing of the area on the night before the Drumcree Church parade is bitterly resented and is seen as preparing the way for yet another Orange parade. Comparisons with events surrounding Civil Rights parades in 1969 become unavoidable, despite the great changes that have taken place within the RUC.

For many nationalists 'Orange' parades are not only symbolic of past oppression but still effectively impose themselves where they are not wanted. Dissatisfaction can reveal itself in a number of ways. Most Catholics, and significant numbers of Protestants, either do their best to ignore the parades, or around the Twelfth, leave Northern Ireland. Others choose actively to protest against the parades, whilst a few get involved in civil disturbances, even attacks on Orange Halls. In recent years there had been regular disturbances on the Garvaghy Road on the night before the Drumcree Church parade. Such disturbances are a clear indication of the tensions that arise over the parades. They are acts of resistance just as much as an organised demonstrations on the road. Only in 1995 were residents groups able to keep the kids off the streets and avoid confrontations with police.

There is also a feeling amongst the protesters that the paramilitary ceasefires was somehow the start of a new era. Some people felt that it was safe to come out and publicly demonstrate against the parades. Prior to the ceasefires there was also concern that people seen protesting at parades might well suffer intimidation at work. For the first time many nationalist residents felt that they could now express their opinions in public and look for 'parity of esteem'.

There is not necessarily agreement amongst residents as to what the future of parades in their area should be. Opposition to the parades is strong, yet there are clearly differences as to exactly what arrangements might be acceptable. Some residents would be happy never to see another Orange parade, while others would concede that, given changed circumstances, they could see Orangemen parading through the area. Also, not surprisingly, in more mixed, or middle class, areas opposition to parades is not as vocal. Nevertheless, there is evidence of a widespread disapproval of certain aspects of parades in both the Catholic and Protestant communities. An opinion poll, commissioned by the *Irish News* last summer, found that 25% of Protestants and 77% of Catholics thought loyalist organisations should not march in nationalist areas. The combined figures showed that 42% of people thought loyalist parades should have the right to march in nationalist areas, 47% thought they should not with 11% don't knows (IN 23-8). A recent community report of the Ballynafeigh area, which is broadly mixed, noted that only 36% of Protestants and 6% of Catholics watched or took part in the parades, while 62% of Protestants and 74% Catholics saw the Twelfth as introducing more tension to the area.

> Most Protestants in the sample remarked that the twelfth was not as well supported as it used to be, that people go on holiday and the area is too tense, especially since the betting shop murders. Some respondents complained of bonfires being built too near houses, or of a younger element indulging in heavy drinking and rough behaviour over the twelfth. Most of the Catholics in the sample remarked on the increased tension and fear during the period. They either went away or stayed indoors until it was all over (Hanlon 1993: 36).

The majority of Protestants questioned highlighted the murders at the bookies on the lower Ormeau as being one of the causes of unease and antagonism, whilst Catholics described their increased fear of intimidation and sectarian attack (Hanlon 1994:35-37). These two examples illustrate that many people from both communities are not keen on parading. In addition to the main issues, they resent the traffic delays and the litter caused by parades, and there are frequent remarks about the way pedestrians are treated if they try and cross a parade. Opposition to particular parades and to parading in general comes from a coalition of a number of different republican and nationalist groups, but also from some in the Protestant community. It is certainly at its most intense within nationalist areas through which parades take place, but there is clearly a more general resentment, in the wider population, of the number of parades and the behaviour of those taking part.

Discussion
Perhaps the area in which there is most misunderstanding of Orangeism amongst residents groups are the motives involved. For many, the actions of those involved in parades are seen as a conspiracy to annoy them with as many parades as possible. The reasons and motivations behind the diverse range of loyalist parades have already been discussed. Those occasions which nationalists feel were deliberate attempts by the Orange Institution to be evasive or deceptive, are often when the tensions between parading groups are revealing themselves. Those representing the Orange Institution in a particular area can only give assurances for particular Orange parades. They often have no authority to act for the Black Institution, and certainly have no authority within the Apprentice Boys or the bands. Those involved in negotiations often have very limited authority and are continually wary of that authority being undermined. Evidence of this can be found in the divisions that have taken place within the Orange Institution which are coalescing under the heading of The Spirit of Drumcree. This group has helped to indicate the wide differences of opinion within Orangeism on, amongst other things, how exactly the disputes over parades should be dealt with.

11.3 Support for loyalist parades in disputed areas
The strongest and more frequent claim for the right to parade is to maintain 'tradition'; namely, that Orangemen should be allowed to parade because it is a significant part of their past, their history and therefore their identity. From this perspective opposition to marches is understood as an attack upon the cultural identity of the marchers, and proof that Irish nationalists are out to destroy all expressions of British, Protestant and Orange culture. In *The Order on Parade* the Grand Lodge defends its position:

> The parades celebrate the Protestant religion and culture and their survival in Ireland. They also celebrate the political and cultural links with mainland Britain which guarantees a pluralist society which can tolerate religious and ethnic diversity as compared with the exclusive nature of the Gaelic/Catholic Irish Republic (Montgomery and Whitten 1995:6)

For many loyalists parading thus becomes emblematic of their attempt to defend themselves from demands for a united Ireland. It is not simply the desire to walk on a particular road but part of a wider territorial dispute.

This perception was taken to its extreme by Ian Paisley in his speech to the rally during the stand-off at Drumcree on 10 July 1995.

> If we cannot go to our place of worship and we cannot walk back from that place of worship then all that the reformation brought to us and all that the martyrs died for and all that our forefathers gave their lives for is lost to us forever. So there can be no turning back. ... And there's a sacrifice to be made by us all and if we don't make that sacrifice our cause will be lost. And if it is lost in Portadown, it's lost, our cause, our county and our future, brethren, is gone from us and we better remember that tonight.

A similar argument was made over the Apprentice Boys parade in Londonderry. Of course, many Orangeman would not take seriously such apocalyptic views over one parade, albeit in the symbolically important locations of Portadown or Londonderry. But the speech does draw upon a general perception that parades are representative of the position loyalists presently feel themselves to be in. These events are not seen in isolation but as part of a general sense of attacks on the Protestant population, including areas like employment and education.

One of the effects of relying upon the use of 'tradition' to legitimise a parade is that re-routing along a non-traditional route could significantly weaken the rights of the Institution in the future. In *The Order on Parade* this particular point is made:

> Agincourt Avenue is neither a traditional route or a main road. To parade along it could lead to parading past Roman Catholic houses - where there has not previously been a parade. Given the political motivation of some people this could have created new problems (Montgomery and Whitten 1995:6).

Once lost, a route might never be regained, but the new route - given that it is not traditional - would be significantly harder to defend. Orangemen in Portadown would still rather parade their traditional route along Obins Street rather than the Garvaghy Road.

The major growth area in parade numbers has probably come from band parades. The legitimisation of these parades is not quite so closely linked with the idea of tradition, although some bands are well established: the Ballynafeigh Apprentice Boys Flute Band is over a hundred years old.

Whilst bands do not always express their right to parade in terms of a traditional route they do see themselves as continuing within a traditional cultural form. Bands and members of the loyal orders see parading as an expression of their cultural identity. Since most of the band-parades do not follow controversial routes their right to parade is less often questioned. There are only a few disputes every year that directly involve band parades.

An argument used in conjunction with that of cultural identity is that the Orange Institution is fundamentally a religious organisation. When the protest is concerned with a church parade, it is perceived, poignantly, as restricting the rights of individuals to go to and from their place of worship. In August, when the Apprentice Boys parade down the Ormeau Road was threatened, some Apprentice Boys in County Down suggested they might blockade Catholic churches. Ironically the local Catholic church in the Ormeau area is at the top of the Ormeau Road, so that some residents of the lower Ormeau go up the road to church. This threat, however, was quickly criticised by the leaders of both the Apprentice Boys and the Orange Institution. Orangemen would argue that the 'civil and religious liberty' they believe in protects everyone's right to proceed to church. The religious rather than political element to Orangeism has been felt so keenly by some, that they have found the overtly political side almost polluting of the religious side. In the 1950s and early 1960s there was a movement in some rural areas, notably in County Antrim, to have no political speeches, and just a religious service at the Twelfth field. To this day there are meetings on the Twelfth that do not have set piece political speeches. The central feature of the Apprentice Boys' parade in August is a service in St. Columb's Cathedral, and there are no political speeches. To many outside, including some Protestants, the idea of Protestant witness is difficult to understand but it does help to explain why church parades are seen as symbolically so important. One Orangeman at a meeting recently pointed out that "Protestantism comes from the word 'protestatio', meaning 'witness' - a stand for something". Orange parades becomes the public expression of those beliefs.

The majority of Orangemen, however, see the disputes as political as much as religious. Whilst Ian Paisley claimed it was an alliance of the Jesuits and Sinn Féin that blocked the Garvaghy Road, most Orangemen would just see the Republican movement or the 'pan-nationalist' front as being to blame. Amongst loyalists on the Ormeau Road, in Portadown, in Castlederg, and in Londonderry it is the activities of Sinn Féin - particularly during the cease-fire - that have heightened tensions over parading. The residents groups are seen as dominated by republican political activists. On the Ormeau Road, the LOCC is seen by loyalists as unrepresentative of the area and responsible for dividing the Ormeau Road into the lower and upper Ormeau. In conjunction with this, the local memory that the area in dispute was largely Protestant, and the belief that they were intimidated out, only hardens the resolve to walk the traditional route. In Portadown, the Garvaghy Road housing is relatively new and was built where there used to be open fields. In Castlederg the area to the north of the town, which is now perceived to be Catholic, was once a venue for the Twelfth. More than one Orangeman has mentioned the possibility that the centre of Belfast will become surrounded by nationalist areas and that the whole Twelfth in Belfast would therefore be brought into question. Give away your rights in one area and they will just attack them in the next. If it's the Ormeau Road this year will it be the Short Strand next year?

Parading disputes can easily be understood in terms of the wider territorial dispute. Areas proclaiming 'No to sectarian marches', like the 'No Go' areas in the early 1970s, are seen as just another diminution of British authority within Northern Ireland. This, of course, is also why the flying of the tricolour is treated with such anger and why most nationalist parades would be unacceptable through loyalist areas or into civic centres. Indeed, one Orangeman who was interviewed suggested that it is the flying of the Union flag that nationalists really object to in an Orange parade. He said he would accept the rights of Catholics to parade up the Ormeau Road as long as the tricolour was not carried. It is important to realise, therefore, that in this sense the dispute over parades is not seen as one of 'rights' or 'parity' but one in which one side's loss is the other side's gain. In these circumstances, compromise becomes perceived as defeat. The resulting celebrations by Unionist politicians when the parade was allowed down the Garvaghy Road on 11 July 1995 was seen as just another indicator of this need to claim victory at all costs.

Some of these more principled arguments are augmented by practical ones. In all the areas where parades have been challenged, concerned loyalists dispute the argument that they set out in some way to disturb, offend or intimidate Catholics. Reference is often made to the 1950s and 1960s when there were very few objections to the parades and Catholics would often come and watch the Twelfth. There seems to be an infinite number of stories of Orangemen sharing their banner poles with Hibernians or an Orange band sharing its instruments with the local Hibernian band

- the conclusion being that if Catholics were not intimidated in the past, then they should not be now. It is also argued that the parades on the disputed routes last a short time, taking only minutes to pass a given point, that they usually take place early in the morning or on a Sunday afternoon, and that most of the routes do not directly pass residential properties. Most of the properties on the Ormeau Road are commercial rather than residential - the houses being on side streets not on the main road. Similarly, the houses on the Garvaghy Road are set well back from the road, there are very few Catholic houses passed by the band parades in Castlederg or Downpatrick, and the walls of Derry are some distance from the Bogside. Orangemen say that they are using the public highway, which they believe they should have every right to use, and, in the case of the Ormeau Road they are using a major road into the city: in short, they believe that residents go out of their way to be disturbed.

Discussion
The area of debate that is perhaps most usefully examined involves the idea of 'tradition'. We would argue that the claim of tradition is both more complex and more dubious than it might at first seem. Perhaps most obviously it relies upon a belief that, because something has tradition, then it is necessarily right. Those in the loyal orders make assumptions about the legitimacy of 'tradition' without ever really explaining why the 'tradition' should be maintained. However, this claim to 'tradition' is also enhanced by a number of other factors. Firstly, and perhaps ironically, many Irish nationalist arguments similarly rely upon the legitimacy of 'tradition' - the legitimacy of the past. Within all sorts of nationalist movements - Irish, British or Ulster - there is an exaggerated importance placed upon the past - it becomes almost sacred. As such, rather than the debate centring upon whether a particular tradition is or is not acceptable as a reason to parade, it instead focuses upon the 'parity of esteem' between 'two traditions'. Secondly the idea of the 'traditional parade' was enshrined in law in the 1951 Public Order Act and used by the police as a legitimate reason for a parade taking place. Although that Act was repealed in 1987 the emphasis on 'traditional' parades remains. In other words, legally 'traditional' parades have been perceived as more legitimate than non-traditional parade which are often regarded as more overtly political. Orange parades have thus been defined as traditional parades not political parades.

There seems to be no clear reason why this should be so. Apart from the route taken, there are many reasons to suggest that much of the content of parades have been recently introduced and in fact are more reflective of present day politics. One might also ask other questions of tradition: When does a parade become 'traditional'? How does one decide what bits of a parade are or are not traditional? What makes a traditional parade so authentic? It is also debatable whether a traditional 'right' necessarily carries precedence over other sorts of 'right'. In other words, the right to parade appears to be treated as greater than the right not to suffer unwanted parades.

Many in the loyal orders also misunderstand the roots of nationalist objections. If members of parading organisations believe that behind the objections to parades is simply a republican plot to destroy Orangeism or 'British culture'; then they are severely underestimating the nature and depth of the resentment that many people feel. That resentment is not just cynically political but is based upon the direct experience that many have had with parades and the historical position of Orangeism within Northern Irish society. When Sinn Féin produce pictures of policeman wearing Orange sashes they may well be dealing in rhetoric, rather than the reality of the present relationship between the Orange Institution and the RUC; nevertheless they are articulating the sense of grievance that many Catholics feel over the involvement of Orangeism in the state of Northern Ireland. For many nationalists, claims by the Orange Institution to be supporters of civil and religious liberty sound rather hollow in the light of the treatment their cultural expression has received when compared to those of the Orange tradition. There has been a restriction on nationalists' right of cultural and political expression in Northern Ireland, although most nationalists see it as another 'Orange parade' amongst a summer of 'Orange parades' and 'Orange parades' are inevitably political. Most nationalists do not expect, indeed, would not want, to see a complete end to Orangeism or to Orange parades. They may not like Orangeism but they would recognise the right of Orangemen to parade, as long as the limitations of those rights were recognised. What nationalists do look for are signs within Orangeism there is some understanding as to why others feel such resentment.

11.4 The Police and Policing
If the police were seen as neutral arbiters in these parading disputes, then their task in controlling the situation would be hard enough. But for both historical and contemporary reasons, the RUC is seen by significant numbers of nationalists as defending a state to which they have no

allegiance. This makes the task of policing parades even more difficult. When the RUC flank a parade through a disputed area they are almost inevitably perceived as defending that unwanted parade. The historical relationship between the police and Stormont, particularly in the late 1960s at the height of the Civil Rights movement, the continuing lack of Catholic recruits to the force, and the overt symbolic displays, such as Union flags outside police stations, all serve to reassert the distrust felt towards the police by a section of the community. This is despite obvious changes that have taken place within the force. The simple fact is that, until there is some agreement on the nature of the state, then any force seen to defend the status quo will be perceived by a section of the community as partial.

This situation has been made yet more complicated by an increase in tension between sections of the Protestant community and the police. This is particularly true in Portadown where the major disturbances that took place in 1985 and 1986 clearly did significant damage to this relationship. It is regularly pointed out in the *Chief Constable's Annual Report*, that parading makes the policing of all the communities in Northern Ireland more difficult.

One of the commonly held suspicions amongst the residents in areas of dispute is that the police and the loyal orders are working together. There are a number of reasons for these suspicions. The majority of police officers are Protestant and they clearly have greater connections with that community. Any police force tends to defend the status quo, and in this case that means defending the historical dominance of the loyal orders in the area of public political expression. Therefore, the RUC seem to facilitate the vast numbers of parades without question, and large numbers of police swamp an area before the parade starts so that residents are hemmed in during the parade. Nevertheless, much of what takes place on the parades suggests that this understanding of the relationship between the security forces and the loyal orders is dated. It is important to remember that the Public Order (NI) Order of 1987 effectively imposed controls on loyalist parades that did not previously exist, and removed the legal protection that 'traditional parades' had been given under previous Stormont legislation. It would now be fairer to say that there can be considerable antipathy between the police and sections of the parade. During the band parade in Downpatrick on 22 October 1995 nineteen different bands walked up to the police lines that blocked the route into the town, and each band taunted the police in turn. A couple of bands hurled fireworks and other objects at the police, who remained disciplined in the front of this largely symbolic onslaught. There have since been charges laid over the incidents. It could of course be asked whether the police would have shown such patience towards a republican parade, but then in that situation the dynamics of mistrust in the relationship are clearly different. However, it is difficult to watch incidents such as this, and the events at Drumcree, and conclude that the loyalist parading organisations have a cosy relationship with the RUC.

In dispelling the idea that the police are somehow facilitating each and every parade, that is not to say that the police have been able to become neutral arbiters. The police still tend to defend the status quo. So, in a town such as Lurgan, with an equal proportion of Protestant and Catholics, the 'traditional' loyalist parades are given access to the town, yet a variety of republican parades are not. Nevertheless, interventions in Portadown in 1985/86, and in the Ormeau Road in 1995/96 amongst others, and the access given to republicans to the centre of Belfast and Castlederg does suggest a willingness on the part of the RUC to change the situation.

The police position on the control of the parades is that they have to be guided by the Public Order (NI) Order 1987. This demands that advance notice of seven days must be given of the route, time, size and organisers of a parade plus the names and numbers of bands taking part. The act allows certain conditions to be imposed on a parade if a senior officer reasonably believes that:

a. it may result in serious public disorder, serious damage to property or serious disruption to the life of the community; or
b. the purpose of the persons organising it is the intimidation of others with a view to compelling them not to do an act they have a right to do, or to do an act they have a right not to do ...

Alternatively, if the situation warrants it, a parade can be banned after referral to the Secretary of State, who normally consults the committee of the Police Authority of Northern Ireland. The Order further deems it an offence to prevent or hinder any lawful public procession or annoy persons taking part in such processions. The Order also prohibits sitting or in any other way obstructing the lawful activity of others, and prohibits the wearing of a uniform signifying association with any political organisation, if the Chief Constable is satisfied that the wearing of such a uniform involves a risk to public order. This law was introduced in the light of the disturbances of 1985 and 1986 in Portadown and is clearly specifically aimed at parade disputes. As with all laws, however, it can be read and used in a variety of ways. Clearly the police can either see the parade as likely to cause the disorder, or the residents demonstration as blocking a legal parade. How does one judge what should be deemed as intimidation?

At many of the disputed parades in 1995 the police waited until the last minute before deciding whether there was likely to be public disorder. Their decision, either to re-route the parade or force it through, apparently depended on which side had amassed the more formidable crowd. The tactic was also used to try and give those mediating the maximum time to get the parties to reach agreement. But its effect was to promote widespread uncertainty. Whilst such decisions are clearly extremely difficult, the result of the tactic they adopted was inevitably to encourage opposed groups to amass as many people on the streets as possible. Consequently, at Drumcree the situation reached a point at which the police appeared stretched to their limits in trying to protect the residents of the Garvaghy Road. Perhaps as a result of this, a month later during the Apprentice Boys parades on the Ormeau Road and on Derry's walls the police appeared to be more determined to make sure the parade got through. This resulted in violent confrontations in both places. Towards the end of the year, the police began to announce decisions on parades a few days before the parade took place. It is a matter of conjecture whether this was because of threatened legal action from the LOCC or whether it was just seen as a tactic less likely to cause a confrontation.

Having made certain criticisms of police tactics however, it is far from clear whether any of the alternative strategies would have achieved more peaceful results. Other options may well have made the situation worse. The conclusion that nearly everyone interviewed had come to is that alternative methods of arbitrating the disputes should be found. Of course, in any future situation the police will have the final say on what takes place but ideally there needs to be action at a community level which relieves the police of having to enforce a relatively arbitrary decision.

11.5 The Media

Clearly the mass media are not to blame for these disputes: nevertheless, much of what fuels the disputes is based upon information which is carried and interpreted by the media. During the course of a number of the interviews it became clear that some reporting by journalists has only served to exacerbate the problem. How does this come about?

Journalists need quick and easy answers, and they are working to deadlines. They are constrained by time, by limited and partial information, by space and by the necessity for simplicity. They are at the mercy of editors, and, to an extent, of politicians. During the events of July 1995 there were complex and sensitive meetings and negotiations taking place in the hope that some sort of resolution could be found on both the Ormeau and Garvaghy Roads. These are situations where any trust at all, built up between interested groups, is inevitably limited. Reports and rumours can quickly undermine confidence. At one public meeting held in late June last year there was some positive discussion between community groups, but the reports the next day took no account of this. Indeed, many of the reporters came into the meeting for a few minutes only to get a sound bite or quote. At Drumcree partial reports based upon inadequate information made the task of mediation significantly harder. On the Ormeau Road, when it appeared that some sort of agreement had been reached, it was during questions on BBC Ulster Radio put to Gerard Rice of LOCC, and Robert Saulters, Belfast County Grand Master, that all the doubts and differences of opinion were made public. The interview was obviously not the only cause of the breakdown, but it certainly facilitated it. Later in the year one newspaper report linked a band parade on the upper part of the Ormeau Road to a commemoration for one of those men believed to be responsible for the Ormeau Road massacre. That same report gave an inaccurate description of the route to be taken by the band parade. Not surprisingly this increased tensions in the area.

    The complex flow of information affects the dynamics of the situation. Rumours and gossip spread quickly, and politicians try to make political capital from the situation. In the field at Drumcree on the evening of 10 July any number of stories as to what the state of play was, spread through the crowd. Some of the misleading stories appear to have been drawn from radio reports. While understanding the need for good, frank, open reporting, much of what takes place falls a long way from this ideal. Coverage of the parades by the media tends to be stereotyped and simplistic. The editorial line taken by the local papers has also tended to entrench positions.

11.6 Conclusions

In asking how and why interpretations of parades differ so widely it is important to remember that the meanings attributable to symbols and events are not simple or stable. An Orange parade means something different to a resident of the Ormeau Road or the Garvaghy Road than it does to an Orangeman, but even within the parades there will be different interpretations. As already pointed out, the political versus the religious role of Orangeism has been much debated within the Institution. Many Orangemen are sincere in their belief that their parades are not intended to offend Roman Catholics. On the other hand, the actions and statements of some Orangemen and non-Orangemen on parades appear to many outsiders to be sectarian. The complex nature of ritual parades allows these things to co-exist.

There is no doubt that there are fundamental differences of opinion on the 'right to parade' which have their roots in the structure of the Northern Ireland conflict. However, there are ways in which the protagonists do understand each other. For example, both sides acknowledge that there is a dispute over territory - which is symbolic of the wider political dispute. To that extent differences in national and religious identification are quite real. But, there are also ways in which the respective groups do not understand each other and consequently interpret each others actions in inaccurate ways. Some of these interpretations may well be politically wilful, others are not. What, therefore, has to be looked at is the possible ways opposing views can be accommodated. Whilst in the short term in are's of dispute this will be extremely difficult, it may well be possible in the medium and long term to produce an environment whereby the likelihood of confrontation is reduced.

SECTION 12: APPROACHES TO RESOLUTION

This section discusses a number of options that have been raised by those involved in some way with the issue of parading as a means of resolving the problem of disputed parades. Some of these could be acted on in the short term, while others would need longer term planning and implementation. These are not recommendations but proposals for discussion. There are no simple answers to these ongoing disputes. Nevertheless, some changes are urgently needed since history tells us that the parading issue is capable of causing major inter-communal civil disturbances.

The control of demonstrations, parades and crowds is not a problem restricted to Northern Ireland but is one that is shared with many societies. For instance, two issues that have been the subject of debate in England over recent years has been controlling the often violent behaviour of football fans and the increasing crowds and disruption at the Notting Hill Carnival. A number of questions have been raised and debated in relation to these events: Who should be responsible for the behaviour of people in public spaces? What rights do those people living adjacent to football grounds and the carnival have? Where does the responsibility of a football club or event organiser finish and those of the police begin? Who should pick up the bill for policing? What is the role of elected representatives in resolving these issues? What public accountability should be expected of people who organise events in public areas? These debates are ongoing although some of the issues have been addressed by Cohen (1993) and by Guilianotti, Bonney and Hepworth (1994). At the heart of all these problems are issues of civil rights. At what point should the rights of the individual to express themselves be seen as secondary to the more general good of the community?

In looking at parades there are a number of issues that need to be approached. There are clearly problems with the issue of traditional rights of way but there are also questions raised about the control of parades, the number of parades and the cost of parades. All these issues have to be weighed against the rights of individuals and groups to political and cultural expression. The ideas discussed below are:

1. The need for negotiation and use of mediation.
2. Guidelines or general principles governing the rights to parade.
3. A parading commission
4. Use of the law.

5. The issue of responsibility - voluntary and imposed constraints on parades.
6. An independent parading tribunal.
7. Parade 'planning permission'.

12.1 Negotiation and Mediation

At present there is no formal mechanism for resolving a parade dispute. Throughout 1995 parade organisers and the protesters were encouraged to discuss the issue among themselves and come to some form of compromise. While this appeared to be an obvious step to most outsiders in fact it proved almost impossible to achieve. To our knowledge it was only on the Ormeau Road that a relatively lengthy period - a number of months - of negotiation, was undertaken. But this persistence was only achieved because of the equally persistent nature of the dispute on the road, and in the end no long term agreement was reached. Elsewhere, where the dispute concerned a single parade the main method of dealing with the tension would probably best be described as crisis management. This was due in part to the fact that parade organisers only need to announce a parade seven days in advance, which does not allow much time for negotiation, in part to the lack of any accepted procedure to adjudicate disputes, except the Public Order Order, and in part to the mutual hostility and suspicion of the opposing parties.

Section Eleven demonstrated there are fundamental differences of perception that make it extremely difficult to reach any agreement. Whilst nationalists read all attempts to parade as part of an ongoing Orange conspiracy to dominate them, loyalists see nationalist objections to parades as part of a wider desire among republican activists to destroy Orangeism. For both sides it is a zero-sum game, a situation where one side will win and the other will lose and therefore it is better to stand one's ground rather than be seen to give any sign of movement. Within the loyalist community, any reduction in traditional parading rights is seen as a further blow in their defence of their British identity. The fears are so great that even those loyalists who do not parade are often prepared to defend the rights of those who do want to parade. As one interested party put it, 'they see the narrow ground as getting narrower'. Even when face to face negotiations have taken place, as on the Ormeau Road, the lack of trust is so great that any agreement that may be reached is in danger of collapse when it is subjected to public scrutiny and outside political pressures. The representatives of the different groups can only sell the agreement to their constituent groups by giving an interpretation that favours their position. This may well be viewed by the other community as a misrepresentation and therefore substantially different from their interpretation of the compromise. In many of these issues the parading disputes are a local reflection of the problems of negotiating the broader peace process.

In practice all attempts to find a compromise demanded the involvement of outside parties acting as some form of mediator. Those involved last year included the Mediation Network for Northern Ireland (Portadown), the Quakers (Ormeau Road), local politicians (Derry, Springfield Road) and the RUC. But third party involvement also raised problems about neutrality and suspicions of a hidden agenda that outsiders may bring with them. Residents groups and those involved in the republican parades remain very suspicious of the motives of the police in general and loyalists are equally suspicious of the residents groups and anyone who is seen to be trying to force them to compromise.

Mediation

In some ways the role of mediation has been misunderstood. In part this is due to the unfamiliarity with the idea and in part due the public way that the Mediation Network for Northern Ireland were involved in the dispute at Drumcree. Mediation is not the same as crisis management Mediation is not about brokering last minute deals or about finding short term solutions that merely displace the problem from today to next week or next year. To be effective, mediation should take place over a longer period of time. In this process the mediators act as a third party to facilitate communication between groups: they discuss the issues in confidence, aim to improve each sides understanding of the other's position and by encouraging creative thinking aim to achieve an acceptable accommodation and resolution to the problem. Mediation can not be imposed on groups, they must we willing and desirous of finding a compromise. Unfortunately when the political heat goes out of the situation, at the end of the marching season, there is little pressure upon interested groups to search for a resolution and diffuse the issue for future years. This is not, we might add, due to a lack of trying by those that have acted as negotiators and mediators.

The different perceptions held by interested parties make any form of mediation difficult, but there are also problems with the role and status of the representatives of those parading and protesting. Loyalist groups do not believe that the leaders or prominent figures in the residents groups represent all the residents of a given area. They have refused to recognise the status of the groups, pointed to the republican background of particular figures and argued that they are no more than Sinn Féin fronts. In each case this is used as a reason not to talk to the residents groups, after all if the leading Unionist politicians refuse to talk to Sinn Féin why should grassroots unionists do so? But there are also problems with the representatives of the loyal institutions. While they have elected officers, in practice these are little more than first among equals, they are not leaders. They can negotiate but they can not agree to a deal. Lodge officials are relatively powerless and this means that they are uncertain of being able to sell any agreement to other members of their organisation. There is a further problem in that lodge officers are elected annually and a deal agreed by officers one year may be rejected by newly elected officials the following year. Furthermore, lodge officers can only negotiate on behalf of their own institution, even if they are a member of other institutions they may have no authority to speak for them. These factors have often confused the issue for nationalists and raised questions of good faith. In fact negotiators on both sides always insist that they must secure agreement for any compromise from a broader constituency. While this is admirably democratic it does pose problems when time is tight. This in turn emphasises the importance of Paisley, and to a lesser extent Trimble, at Drumcree. They had the status to negotiate an agreement, but they also had the authority to bring the crowd along with them. Elsewhere, deals agreed through third parties were always subject to subsequent ratification by residents groups or loyal orders. This took time and offered no certainty of success.

A further complication in the process of mediation is that any agreement inevitably needs to be underwritten by the RUC. Given the level of distrust with which the RUC are held, in particular by nationalists, problems can also arise over who will guarantee that the deal is honoured. It becomes almost inevitable that overtime those involved in negotiation and mediation are also pulled in to the environment of mistrust. It becomes increasingly hard for them to be seen as honest brokers as the results of attempts to negotiate became public. If the perceptions remain that loyalists will lose something or that nationalists will be expected to compromise too far then they become less inclined to talk to intermediaries in the first place.

The work done by intermediaries up to this point has only served to indicate the desperate need for a more general approach to the problem.

If those outside the disputes are expecting the Mediation Network for Northern Ireland, the Quakers, or any other intermediary to come up with an overall answer then they are going to be disappointed. Whilst they can be of great assistance in specific areas, no amount of honest intentions, skill, time and patience on behalf of these people will overcome the wider problems of mistrust and a lack of desire to compromise. Indeed, if the parading disputes continue at their present level and resentment increases, it may well become harder not easier, to find negotiated accommodation.

12.2 Guidelines for Parades
One attempt to overcome the present piecemeal approach to parade disputes has been made by the Lower Ormeau Concerned Community. They produced a set of general guidelines, in February 1996, which they would like to apply to all public demonstrations. Their six guidelines are:

1. The Public Order legislation is a totally inadequate way of dealing with the issue of parades.
2. People have the right to march, but that right is not unconditional and must be exercised with consideration for the rights and sensitivities of others.
3. The residents of areas through which parades intend to pass have the right to withhold their consent to those parades if they feel the parades are offensive.
4. In general, people should have the right to parade in the commercial centres of villages, towns and cities. However, loyalist parades should avoid villages and towns which are overwhelmingly nationalist and nationalist parades should avoid villages and towns which are overwhelmingly loyalist or unionist.
5. Traditional march routes can and will change over time to take into account demographic changes in the population living along those routes.
6. March organisers must give assurances about the behaviour of marchers and those who associate themselves with marches, and must ensure that sectarian provocation is avoided. Permission for future marches should be dependent on those assurances being fulfilled.

The LOCC believe that the adoption of these principles would protect 'the right to march' and also protect communities from 'tension, fear and provocation'. They assert the rights of all groups to use the commercial centres of villages, towns and cities, but point out that such rights are not unconditional. They claim that traditional parades can not override the rights of communities but that demographic changes have to be taken into account. Furthermore parade organisers must give assurances over the behaviour of those taking part while permission for future parades would be dependent upon that good behaviour.

The LOCC principles cover a number of issues. The legal issues will be examined in section 12.4, and the issue of behaviour and responsibility considered in sections 12.5 and 12.7.

Consent or Consensus
The principle of consent is at the heart of the LOCC argument. The LOCC state that parade organisers must have the consent of those communities through which the parades pass. A report produced by the Pat Finucane Centre put forward similar recommendations. The Garvaghy Road Residents Group and some loyalist residents who object to nationalist parades have also made this argument. Nationalist parades were regularly stopped under Stormont using much the same reasoning. Indeed, one could argue that the state of Northern Ireland was also set up using similar principles: the majority in the six counties, would not give their consent to Home Rule and demanded a separate state. And, furthermore, the Framework Document and the Downing Street Agreement use the idea of consent in a number of contexts.

The principle of consent is central to the workings of democracy, and yet it is far from a simple principle to apply. In what areas should consent be sought? How often should consent be sought? How should consent be tested - by survey, by local referendum, by public meeting - and who should test it? At what point should it be deemed that an area no longer consents to a parade taking place - when 50% of the population are against it or should it be 75% or more? Consent may well be an important principle for judging the merits of parades but it must be realised that it is not simple to put into practice. Not only are the mechanics of such a form of local democracy not in place at present but it is not easy to see when they would ever be put in place.

The LOCC principles suggest that the consent of the residents is an absolute requirement before a parade or political event can take place in, or near, any area. The introduction of such a principle based upon local community groups could have far reaching, long term, effects, for open political expression. Therefore, a revision to such a principle might emphasise that whilst communities do not have an absolute right to veto the political expression of others, their feelings should play an important role in any considerations that are made. It is important to remember that the annual recurrence of many loyalist parades developed in the last 100 years when the absolute right of the loyal orders to parade, whenever and wherever they wanted, was rarely if ever questioned. Crucially, similar rights of expression were not afforded to the nationalist community. Put simply, in the area of public political expression there was clear discrimination. It could, therefore, be argued that whilst absolute rights of veto would not create a healthy democratic climate there is still a continuing imbalance of political expression, albeit as a legacy from past political structures as well as continuing political divisions. Under new conditions therefore it might be argued that no Orange parade necessarily has the right to take place, however 'traditional' they may be, since those 'traditional' rights were based upon a grave imbalance of power. But it might also be argued that no Orange parade can necessarily be excluded exclusively on the principle that local consent has not been gained. In the same way, loyalist communities do not have the absolute right to exclude demonstrations from their areas and particularly from town centres. Perhaps it would be of more use to talk in terms of 'consensus', rather than 'consent', when examining the right to parade, this in turn would re-emphasise the need for ongoing dialogue between the opposing parties. However, at the moment consensus has connotations of compromise which neither side wishes to make.

The LOCC principles have received a broad acceptance within the nationalist community but there have been no formal responses to them from within the unionist community. These principles may well be able to be used as the basis for a more widely accepted series of guidelines, but they would need the acceptance of the unionist community to be workable. The questions that we have raised over the issue of consent illustrates some of the questions that would need to be addressed to achieve a more broadly acceptable series of guidelines for parades.

12.3 A Parading Commission

One way of exploring and developing the idea of a set of general principles, and taking a broader view of the entire issue of parades would be to establish a Parading Commission. The idea of a commission has already been used to try to overcome difficulties in the peace process regarding the decommissioning of weapons, while the earlier Opsahl Commission had a much wider ranging brief with regard to the political stalemate in the north. A Parading Commission could be set up with a specific brief and a clear timetable, it could be asked to draw up a broadly acceptable series of guidelines which both parade organisers and protesters would be expected to follow. As an extension it could also be asked to make a series of recommendations as to how the existing disputes might be resolved.

A parading commission could either be made up of neutral or independent parties, or it could include representatives of both communities under an independent chair. In either case the commission could take submissions from all those with an interest in the issue. The commission could evaluate the general ideas that have been addressed by the LOCC but it could also address some of the more practical constraints that are regularly imposed on parades, and consider whether they might be more generally applied (see 11.6). It could consider the more abstract principles of 'consent' and 'tradition' and evaluate the arguments between the 'right to parade' and the 'right not to suffer parades', which are so often invoked but have not been examined in detail. The commission would then produce a set of general guidelines upon which the right of public political expression could be based (see Bryson and McCartney 1994: 154-156 for a similar suggestion).

The commission could also be asked to address the specific parades that have been opposed in recent years and perhaps offer a blue-print for the forthcoming marching season. Although it would only have an advisory role, and the final decisions would be left to the RUC, the commission could offer an overview and make some suggestions on how each of the parades in Belfast, Bellaghy, Derry, Downpatrick, Dunloy, Lurgan, Portadown, Rosslea and other places might be approached. But it would present the suggestions as a package, addressing the marching season as a single extended event. Such an overview might suggest a different pattern from the present one whereby each dispute is seen as another step on a one way path of gains or losses.

There could be a number of advantages to a commission:

1. It could be established relatively quickly and easily and without legislation.
2. It could be given a limited timescale and be expected to report early next year.

3. It would stimulate a public debate on the issue of parades outside of the marching season.
4. It could offer a blueprint for addressing the ongoing disputes.
5. It would create a widely agreed set of principles which apply to both parade organisers and protesters.
6. The issue would be addressed by force of argument rather than force of numbers.

The commission then could work on the same principles as mediation and negotiation. It would try to seek a workable compromise over the general right to parade and it could advise, or make recommendations, on specific disputes. The failure of any of the local level attempts at compromise may imply that a commission would have no more success. However, the very fact that it would provide an overview which would include all current disputes may mean that each side would see both gains and losses emerging from the process and we could thereby move away from the zero-sum game.

While the aim of the commission would be to address some of the immediate issues surrounding parades, it could also be asked to evaluate some of the longer term ideas, such as a permanent tribunal, more formal 'planning permission' and changes to the legislation which we discuss below.

12.4 Use of the Law
The first of the six LOCC principles states that they consider the existing public order legislation to be inadequate. It has also been suggested by other parties that new legislation may be required to resolve the issue of parading rights. The authors of this study have no legal expertise and can only make very general points; it may well be that some of the options discussed below would require a legal basis and therefore new legislation. At the time of writing there has been no suggestion that a change in legislation is being actively considered. One alternative option, however, might be to examine the way the present legislation is being used.

Despite their criticism of present legislation, the LOCC have been willing to use legal means in an attempt to have injunctions placed on parades along the Ormeau Road. At the same time the preamble to the LOCC principles also emphasises the need to deal with the 'tension, fear and intimidation' that may accompany parades. Only Part II of the Public Order (NI) Order 1987, which is concerned with 'Processions and Meetings' has been invoked in the current dispute, but Part III of the act deals with 'Acts intended or likely to stir up hatred or arouse fear' which LOCC say is a large part of the problem.

Given the nature of the state of Northern Ireland since its foundation and the persistent violence of the past thirty years, then many of the symbols that appear in loyalist and republican parades can and will arouse fear in the other community. A UVF or Republican flag can appear threatening, many of the songs, tunes and chants that are part of the 'folk' cultures in both communities can be perceived as intimidating. This situation can only be alleviated over the course of time. However, a greater understanding of those fears from parade organisers could be reflected in the actions of those on parade in sensitive areas. Alternatively, this approach may demand the more robust policing of sectarianism in public demonstrations. The problem with this approach is always the judgement of intimidation. Article 9, Paragraph 4 of the Public Order Order indicates that intent has to be proved. Prosecution in such cases is notoriously difficult and this is perhaps why the legislation is not widely used (see Bryson and McCartney 1994:144-156 for a more detailed discussion on the Public Order Order).

Nevertheless, difficult though it might be, perhaps it is time for judgements to be made on the broader issue of public behaviour at parades. Some aspects that could be considered are fairly obvious. They include the general behaviour of both those on parade and spectators including 'hangers on', the music that is played and the chanting that accompanies particular music, the flags and banners that are carried, the size and length of the parade as well as its make up and the reason for the parade. Many of these have already been subject to both police and voluntary constraints and will be considered in more detail in the next sections.

12.5 Responsible Parading

It is sometimes forgotten that despite the ethnically divided nature of residential areas across Northern Ireland, all areas are still, to some extent, mixed. Almost all residential areas include some Catholics or some Protestants, almost all areas contain people who consider themselves British and people who consider themselves Irish. The issue of responsibility is not only about the conduct of Orange parades on the Ormeau Road or republican parades in Suffolk but also the conduct of parades in currently uncontentious areas such as Banbridge or Crossmaglen. The object of controls is not to mute a political position but to reduce the overt threat to others. One feature of a set of broad guidelines could focus attention on the need for parade organisers to take greater responsibility for the totality of the event.

One recent example can illustrate the argument. The Orange Order has claimed that the bands were a key factor in the increase in problems at parades (Montgomery and Whitten 1995:34-35), to an extent this was also implicit in an earlier report produced by the Centre for the Study of Conflict (Bryan, Fraser and Dunn 1995). While the rise of blood and thunder bands is partly responsible for the increase in the number of parades and their overt sectarian nature, it is parades organised by the loyal orders that have caused most controversy. Even in those cases where bandsmen have been prominent in causing trouble it is Orange lodges that have given support to the bands by hiring them, and it is Orangeism which is perceived as the cultural root of parading by those outside the institutions. It is not adequate to say 'we can not control the bands' or 'we are not responsible for the people on the pavements'. Parade organisers should recognise that they must take responsibility for all aspects of the parade and all those features that might cause offence or disturbance to other people. The loyal orders have a wide range of rules and regulations which the participants of parades are expected to follow: they provide marshals or stewards at parades, they demand that bands being hired sign a contract, and they do - on occasions - take actions if members or bands transgress the rules. However, the recognition that greater consideration should be given to the total content of parades, which is made by Montgomery and Whitten, can only prove of real benefit to the public perception of the Order if these rules and constraints are known to those outside the parading body. The loyal orders have taken many steps to address criticism of their parades, part of the problem is that they have failed to publicise these acts for fear of being seen to compromise with protesters (specific constraints on parades are considered in more detail in section 12.7 below). It is not just a matter of imposing rules and regulations on a parade, it is also important to be seen to do so.

How could parade organisers take greater responsibility for their parades? Some of these matters could be dealt with swiftly and voluntarily, while others may need to be imposed on parade organisers.

General Behaviour
The situation at parades could be improved by some relatively simple measures. Parade organisers could publicise what sort of behaviour is and

is not acceptable on parades. Sectarian chanting, the carrying of threatening symbols, playing louder in front of churches, the taunting of crowds - no matter what the provocation - should all be specifically dealt with. Many of these activities are already covered by rules of the loyal orders, but the suspicion remains that their enforcement is haphazard and often non-existent, and that little responsibility is taken for spectators or 'hangers on'. Some members of the loyal orders do put considerable time and effort into trying to ensure that parades are disciplined and peaceful. Nevertheless, parades are often high spirited occasions which involve a collection of disparate groups and individuals and which also attract a less controllable range of spectators.

Stewarding or Marshalling

To implement more control over the general behaviour of all people at parades would require an extensive use of stewards, who were clearly designated to do that job. At football grounds the stewards are expected to watch the spectators at all times; this means that they are not watching the game. At present most of the stewards at Orange parades are largely indistinguishable from the rest of the people on parade and indeed they often walk with the parade. Whilst at smaller events stewards may need to walk alongside the parade, for the larger parades more stewards may be required and they could be made responsible for a defined stretch of road or area. These stationary stewards could be expected to control pedestrians, spectators and traffic in a more organised manner than the rather haphazard way that parades are marshalled at present. Any incidents should be reported and dealt with in accordance with the guidelines the organising institution has laid down. If those organising the parade were unable to satisfy the police that the event would be adequately controlled then permission for the parade could be refused. If stewarding at the parade proved inadequate then questions would be raised over the organisers right to parade in the future. It might even be worth considering some sort of training for stewards.

Community Liaison

Stewards could also be expected to liaise closely with, and function as a contact for people from the local community. At present it is often difficult for residents to find the appropriate person to deal with in any of the loyal orders. Matters might improve if there was better liaison with local community groups. Information about when and where parades are taking place is often hard to come by. This may well be because organisers fear for the security of the parade. In a situation where the security risk has been reduced it would be advantageous for a community to be aware that a parade is going to take place and how long it would last. Areas of particular sensitivity along a parade route, such as nationalist estates, churches or hospitals could demand more extensive stewarding or could involve stewards from both communities. Cooperative stewarding could eventually reduce the scale of the police presence that is currently deemed necessary. A liaison officer within each organisation could also deal with complaints about behaviour on the parade from residents, and could inform the complainants what action had been taken. All these matters would increase the public accountability of parade organisers and perhaps help to allay some of the general suspicion felt in nationalist communities towards Orange parades.

Voluntary Re-routing
The ultimate voluntary constraint is to decide not to parade along a particular route. Such action need not preclude that route from being used in the future, but simply accepts that given present community sensitivities, and given the historical resonance of parades, an alternative route should be taken. Such situations already exists in a number of areas in Northern Ireland - areas where it would be seen as quite impractical for loyalist or republican parades to go. In a number of the current disputed areas, residents have suggested that re-routing need not be permanent, but a voluntary re-routing would be seen as an act of good faith, and a step towards addressing real concerns.

Externally Imposed Constraints
As well as actions the organisers of parades might undertake to control behaviour, there may also be statutory ways in which the control of parades might be improved. At the moment the RUC can, and do, impose a range of constraints on parade organisers (see 12.7). It may well be within the remit of an independent commission or tribunal to explore the range of possible constraints more fully. It is here that the comparison with English football crowds becomes interesting. There has been considerable pressure placed upon English football clubs to control their own supporters, which has not always been an easy proposition. Many clubs feel they have been made responsible for things that are more to do with the ills of society than with football. Nevertheless, over the last fifteen years all football clubs have been forced to take greater responsibility

for the control of spectators at their ground. This was forced upon them by a combination of legislation, the financial penalties of falling gates, and punitive penalties introduced by authorities, such as UEFA and the FA. Most clubs are also actively involved in schemes to reduce racism at matches and there appears to be a growing awareness in Glasgow that sectarianism in the football culture of the city needs to be dealt with. Reduced intimidation at football grounds has, in England at least, played a part in increasing the crowds going through the gates.

Are there any lessons this example could teach us? Parades take place on open public streets not enclosed grounds. However, the organisers of parades have authority over the proceedings and should be expected to take more responsibility for what takes place during the parades. At present we have a situation where groups appear to be 'parading without responsibility': if trouble occurs the blame is often laid elsewhere.

Financial Responsibility

One recent constraint imposed on football clubs in England is to pay for the costs of providing adequate policing. It has been mooted that parade organisers should be responsible for the costs of policing parades in Northern Ireland. The RUC *Chief Constable's Annual Report* regularly notes the drain on resources resulting from intensive policing of parades. The cost of policing the events of July last year alone was estimated to be over £2 million. Clearly, expecting parade organisers to pay for all policing costs would be prohibitive. However, one suggestion made in the course of this study was that organisers could be asked to put up a bond, or take out insurance, against damage or violent behaviour. It is not unusual for groups and organisations who utilise the public areas, such as race organisations, motorists, building contractors; to cover themselves for financial liabilities. Of course there might be issues of which complicate determination of liability: provocative behaviour from opponents of a parade, or agents provocateurs. Nevertheless, such a financial requirement might force parade organisers to be more aware of the wider implications of their actions.

Summary

These are possible ways through which much of the tension that builds up over parades could be addressed before it erupts into violence. These suggestions ask questions of those organising the parades and in practice will make greater demands upon the way they run their parades. Indeed, this might mean that fewer parades are organised, but the result of that may also be to improve the climate in which parades take place, to reduce the amount of policing that needs to take place, and eventually to make parades more acceptable to the wider community. Those rules that already exist over parades need to be made more public and better enforced and serious consideration would need to be given to a new set of guidelines. Those guidelines might, for instance clearly stipulate the actions of those on the parade when in the area of a Roman Catholic church, even in predominantly Protestant areas, routes might be redesigned to avoid Catholic churches. These sorts of measures were not uncommon in the 1950s and 1960s and are still used in some localities at the present. But there are clearly areas where voluntary changes would be welcomed and could ease tension. It should be clear that these changes will not solve immediate problems but would hopefully reduce the amount of problems in the future. Nevertheless, much of the initiative in this area needs to come from the organisers of parades.

12.6 A Parading Tribunal
If a directly negotiated compromise is widely regarded as the ideal means of resolving the disputes, the failure of disputants to agree to talk to each other has led to widespread suggestions that an independent body should be set up to adjudicate on the matter. This idea was suggested by the then Chief Constable, John Hermon, in his Annual Report of 1985. In an interview in the *Belfast Telegraph* he offered some elaboration on his thinking:

> My inclination, and it is coming round to a firm view, is that it would be better to have an independent body examine the propriety of a parade being allowed into a certain area. The police could refer any notice of a contentious parade to a tribunal. They would state their views as professional police officers and the organisers would be able to present their case in justification. Local people through their representatives, could express their view (BT 1-5-86).

There seems to be no precedent for such a body dealing with parades or other forms of public political expression. However, given the large numbers of parades every year, the continuous growth in numbers and the increasing costs and disruption they can cause there is a good argument for an independent body to oversee all parades. A comparison can be made with the area of employment which has been subject to legislative constraints. Laws governing equal opportunities and fair employment practices as well as tribunals for the redress of unfair dismissal or industrial disputes are common to most modern western societies. Whilst the need for such laws and bodies is probably universally accepted, they are also often treated with suspicion. This has been particularly true in Northern Ireland where many Protestants see the fair employment system as inevitably reducing their chances of employment. Nevertheless, employment practices are not as politically contentious as they were thirty years ago and, despite criticisms, progress has been made in redressing the balance between employment opportunities between the two communities (FEC Annual Report 1996, IN 29-3-96, Sheehan 1995). Could the area of public parades benefit from similar legislation and structures?

The idea of a parading tribunal has received support from many quarters, but little flesh has been put on the bones of this idea. This section suggests possible ways in which a tribunal might operate. Other possible structures might be possible. Again, these ideas are offered as a stimulus to further discussion.

A Judicial Tribunal

Any tribunal that would to be expected to impose rulings on parade disputes would require a legal status and a formal authority. At the same time, to be widely accepted, and therefore to be successful, it would also need a substantial degree of legitimacy from among the population of Northern Ireland. A voluntary body might be useful in encouraging negotiation and general discussion of the many connected issues and it may provide a forum in which voluntary guidelines for parading and protesting may be agreed (see 12.3), but without legal status such a body would only be able to advise on disputes and would not be able to impose decisions.

A tribunal would need authority to underwrite its decisions and would also need to be recognised as even handed and independent. How does one ensure that such a body can seen as independent and yet have some power? On the one hand, nationalists would expect such a body to be as far removed form the forces of the state as possible, before they could put any faith in it. On the other hand, to have practical power, and to gain the acceptance of many in the loyalist community, it would need to be set up within existing legal and policing structures. Clearly, any direct involvement either by the police or by government officials would be problematic. However, the present willingness of some of the residents groups to take legal action in advance of their demands suggests that they do see the judiciary as having some independence from other forces of the state. Possibly, therefore, a panel which is chaired by a member of the judiciary with wide civil rights experience might have some hope of being accepted.

A judicial tribunal could be brought into play over contentious parades. It could be asked to deliberate on the matter by the police or by the Secretary of State. It could take evidence from all interested parties before arriving at a decision. Its decision could be forwarded to the Secretary of State who might then act on it, in which case the decision would ultimately be a political one. Or its authority could have the force of law and the police would be expected to proceed according to the tribunal's decision.

Local Committees
It has been suggested that one of the problems of a judicial tribunal might be that it would pay insufficient consideration to local particularities. Therefore, any such system might be set up on a more local basis. This would entail community representatives coming together to make decisions on how particular local parades should be dealt with. One obvious group of representatives that might be used in this situation are local councillors, since, in theory at least, local councillors that have a democratic mandate to represent the people in their particular area. They may well be able to represent the views of those not taking to the streets to march or protest. A number of groups have criticised the apparent lack of involvement of local councillors in the ongoing disputes, although we are aware of some exceptions. Perhaps local committees could be formed from councillors, church leaders, representatives of local community groups, residents and parade organisers to try and resolve problems. Solutions that appear from this sort of base would have advantages over those imposed from outside and could make the work of policing easier. Unfortunately, recent experience suggests that such local committees are difficult to organise. The repercussions of a lack of community agreement is that decisions would have to be imposed from above. It is of course possible that such local initiatives that do develop could be represented in the wider processes. Alternatively, it may be better to devise a system with that includes both local representatives and a more removed, neutral chairperson.

Public Order vs. Civil Rights

Clearly, in any future situation, direct policing of all public demonstrations will always be necessary and certain decisions will always have to be made by police officers. However, as things stand the only principles the RUC have to work with are those enshrined in the Public Order Order. These effectively ensure that the keeping of public order is the only priority on which the police can act. As a result, decisions are made that appear quite at odds with ideas of 'rights' and 'justice'. As it stands republicans are allowed to parade into the centre of Belfast but they are not allowed into the centre of Lurgan. The Apprentice Boys were allowed to parade along the lower Ormeau Road so that they can board a bus in the city centre which will take them to a parade 80 miles away, but Orangemen were not allowed to walk the same route to join the VE Day commemorations in the city centre. A number of church parades, which normally attract little interest are stopped at the Ormeau Bridge whereas the larger Twelfth parade which causes major inconvenience is allowed to take place. Orangemen are allowed to parade in Downpatrick town centre, whereas a local band is not. Whilst the necessity for pragmatic policing decisions will never be completely removed it would seem reasonable that a system might be introduced on which more consistent decisions could be made. A tribunal could therefore be expected to take a much wider range of factors into consideration when arriving at its decision. Such a procedure could address a number of issues that are regularly seen as problems in the present method of deciding whether a parade should go ahead. These include:

1. The decision could be based on a wide range of issues rather than just public order.
2. The reasoning behind the decision would be made public.
3. The police would no longer be responsible for deciding whether a parade should proceed or not.
4. It would also be clear in advance of the parade whether the organisers or protesters had the law on their side.
5. Decisions could be made about a number of parades well in advance. For instance a tribunal could decide on whether any parades should be allowed along the lower Ormeau Road, and if so which ones.
6. There would be time, and a procedure, to appeal against a decision.

In general, a tribunal of some kind would make the issue of parades the subject of debate and of reasoned argument. It would bring the issue into the public domain and ensure that the outcome was open to public scrutiny.

12.7 Parade 'Planning' Permission

The idea of a tribunal has been considered in relation to disputed parades. However, a more formal system might be constructed along the principles of planning legislation which would be applied to all parades. Such a procedure would reinforce the fact that all parades impose to a greater or lesser extent on a community. It would reinforce the idea that organisers have a responsibility for the parade in its broadest impact. The idea of some form of 'planning permission' would be an extension of the current system whereby parade organisers inform the police of their intention of holding a parade seven days in advance. As with the current procedure, most parades would be agreed with no controversy and a minimum of fuss. But a more open system would give people more information about parades planned for each area.

A formal application to hold an annual parade would have to be made well in advance of the parade and the information about all planned parades in an area would be made public. This could be done by publishing the details in a local newspaper and listing them in a public place.

When the demand for seven days notice for all parades was introduced in 1987 it was greeted with protests, but increasing the notice should not cause practical problems to parade organisers since the dates of most parades are known well in advance. Would it be unreasonable to require parade organisers to advise of their parades three months or even six months in advance? Or even require them to list all the parades and their routes at the beginning of each year? Obviously there would need to be a 'fast track' procedure for 'single issue' parades but since these tend to be less controversial that should not be too great a problem.

If most parades are traditional and unchanging it is difficult to see the objections and there may well be hidden benefits for parade organisers. One of the complaints raised by residents is that there are always new parades being 'invented' or that parades take them by surprise. Last year there was considerable confusion over the number of parades that would be going down the Ormeau Road. Publicising the dates of parades, the probable size, the likely time the parade would take place and the reasons for the parade may well go some way to increasing a wider understanding of loyalist parades and dispelling the suspicion and confusion that arises through misinformation. If nothing else it could be seen as gesture of goodwill which costs nothing.

Constraints and Objections
At present parade organisers sometimes appear to have an unconstrained right to hold a parade whenever they wish, but as the number of parades grows they impinge more frequently on those who do not parade. Constraints, responsibilities and requirements are formally imposed on a range of activities that once were unregulated: cycle races and motor races both require permission to dominate the public roads and while they are very different from parades, parade organisers should at very least recognise their responsibility to the broader sphere of civil society. Notification and a formal request for permission would be an acknowledgement that parades impose upon other people to some extent. At the moment there is no indication of the degree of support for, or opposition to, parades in many areas and in the vast majority of cases request for a parade could easily be dealt with by a tribunal.

Such a system would also allow any objections to a parade to be heard and considered, in confidence if necessary. It would give an insight into a range of attitudes to parades and might allow complaints to be dealt with before they become major issues. Having requested permission, the organisers could make their case, any opponents could state their objections, the RUC could offer their assessment and the tribunal could adjudicate. In such a system both the arguments, the reasoning and the conditions or terms of permission would be open to public scrutiny. Conditions may be imposed so that parades would not be allowed into particular areas. However, there may be no need to stop particular parades or even reduce the number of parades but simply need to ensure that organisers accept their responsibility to the wider community. By making the decision well enough in advance there would also be time for appeals to be made if the decision was felt to be unfair in any way.

Imposing Conditions
The decision to allow a parade, to reroute a parade or to impose other conditions on the organisers could be based on a broad range of considerations. These could include such factors as the willingness to enter discussions or to offer concessions, either by objectors or organisers; the conduct at previous events or agreeing to abide by conditions imposed; the changes in local conditions or if the political situation dictates that

tensions are particularly high then that also could be taken into consideration. A broad range of restrictions or conditions could also be placed upon events.

In 1995 most emphasis was placed on the rerouting of parades, but the RUC can and do demand a range of specific conditions on parade organisers. In some cases the loyal orders have imposed restraints on themselves. Often these conditions are not publicised, but this is a double-edged sword. On the one hand some loyalists would argue that agreeing to any constraints is a denial of their rights, but on the other hand failing to publicise voluntarily imposed constraints can suggest a lack of willingness to compromise and fail to show goodwill where it does exist. For example the Apprentice Boys voluntarily imposed a number of constraints on bands and regalia to ensure they were allowed to parade the city walls in Derry last summer and the local Belfast Walker Club have long restricted the flags they carry along the Ormeau Road. However, in both cases the impact of these self-imposed restrictions was lost because they were not announced publicly.

The sorts of constraints that have either been offered or imposed by the loyal orders in recent disputes include:

1. rerouting some parades along a route in return for a guarantee that others will be allowed;
2. rerouting the return leg of a parade;
3. furling flags;
4. restricting the range of flags;
5. restraining the number of bands on the parade;
6. restraining the type of bands on parade;
7. restraining the type of music played;
8. walking in silence;
9. parading early in the morning;
10. restricting access to parts of the route to supporters.

Any of these constraints can be imposed voluntarily by parade organisers or they could be imposed by an outside authority. Voluntary constraint has often been concealed from the public debate because it is perceived to be an act of weakness, to be a response to pressure from the other side. But there is another side to this argument. Voluntary restraints can also be imposed from a position of strength, they can be a recognition that a complaint has some validity and must be addressed. As part of a zero-sum game a constraint is seen as a loss, in a more open system a voluntarily imposed constraint can be seen as an attempt to improve a situation and to work towards a more widely acceptable means of maintaining and developing cultural traditions.

Guaranteeing the Right to Parade
The imposition of constraints on a parade need not be seen as a one-way street, but as a way of neutralising a dispute and preparing the way for better mutual understanding. Part of the problem at present is that all concessions are seen as part of a wider attack on loyalist parades, and that any concessions will lead to yet more demands in the future. Independent arbitration may be able to guarantee future rights, impose constraints for a limited period or reverse restrictions.

The members of the LOCC have suggested that they might be willing to accept parades in the future, but present lack of trust undermines such an offer. An independent body could provide longer term guarantees that concessions were not a one-way street. It could evaluate ongoing discussions, it could suggest that constraints are imposed for one, two or more parades or that they would be reviewed the following year. The body could also suggest parameters for protesters and impose demands or conditions on the ways that parades are challenged. By introducing such a system it may be possible that it is the force of argument and the ongoing behaviour of both parade participants and protesters that are considered in deciding on the propriety of a parade and not the weight of numbers on the day. The police would be seen to be acting on a publicly recognised agreement. Importantly, if one particular group uses force in a given situation then that may well prejudice future decisions. The right to parade or to protest at parades would therefore be balanced by the demand for responsibility to the wider society.

The Rights of Residents
We have tried to suggest ways in which parading may be made more acceptable to as many people as possible, and we have suggested ways that parade organisers may seek to address the complaints of residents when parades pass in, or near, nationalist areas. However, one must also acknowledge that any number of concessions may still fail to make parades acceptable to residents; that past hurts are still too raw and that the only compromise that goes far enough may be for the parade organisers to re-route their parade away from the area in question. Such a re-routing need not be seen as permanent. It could remain for a set number of years and might be linked to local community education programmes. The members of the LOCC have left the door open to the loyal orders to come

into their community and begin to build trust. In the immediate future it would seem that steps towards a resolution of the parading issue would have to be addressed at both local level and through more wide-ranging initiatives.

12.8 Conclusions

In looking for ways in which to produce a better environment for public political expression a number of levels have been considered, ranging from the practical local short term measures to more abstract notions of collective and individual rights and responsibilities. None of the suggestions that have been discussed would be easy to implement without the good will of communities, nor would they necessarily have an immediate effect. The idea of an independent body to address the issue is currently gaining substantial support. We have tried to flesh out some parameters for discussion and raise some of the potential pitfalls.

One interested individual has suggested that anyone adjudicating over a disputed parade would require 'the wisdom of Solomon'. There would be awkward judgements to be made on a whole range of issues. However, many of those judgements are, in effect, already made but the process is never public and the principles are never clear.

These ideas discussed above may have been suggested too late to resolve the immediate disputes. As with the introduction of the Public Order Order in 1987, any attempts to find long term solutions may well cause a number of short term problems. Whilst better control of parades could be forced upon organisations, there are a number of suggestions through which they could voluntarily improve their own control mechanisms, even suspend parades in an area for a particular length of time. The long term result of these measures would be to make parade organisers more responsible and accountable for the events they organise. The aim is not to prevent parades from taking place but rather to encourage a political environment where civil rights are respected and political and religious expression can take place without threatening or inconveniencing the lives of others.

PART FOUR - REVIEW

SECTION 13: THE DISPUTED AREAS

BELFAST, Ormeau Road: The protest is organised by the Lower Ormeau Concerned Community (LOCC) which was formed by residents of the area from the Ormeau Bridge to Cooke Street on the eastern side of the Ormeau Road and those in the McClure Street area. The LOCC object to the numerous loyalist parades along the Ormeau Road which the say are often intimidating and they regard as an offensive display of triumphalism. They argues that (a) several of the parades only walk along the lower Ormeau to meet a bus in the city centre and the men could board the bus at the Annadale Embankment instead and (b) alternative return routes have already been adopted on some parades and these could be used regularly. In a recent press release the LOCC suggested that as a general principal all parades should seek permission from the residents of the areas on their route, rather than assuming that tradition gives them an automatic right to parade.

As a secondary issue, the LOCC criticised the scale of policing that is imposed for major parades. Residents feel that they are subject to a curfew at such times. On the two occasions when parades were forced through in 1995 they claim the problems were exacerbated by the intense police presence, the blocking off of all side roads and commercial premises and restrictions on personal movement.

Officials of the loyal orders argue that the Ormeau Road is the main thoroughfare from Ballynafeigh into the city centre and it is the most direct route. They also note that parades have been using this route for nearly a century. They argue that the parades are not meant to be offensive, that the majority of parades involve members going to church, that constraints have been imposed on the bands and that those individuals who behaved badly in 1992 have all been disciplined. They further note that the parades are held either early in the morning or on a Sunday afternoon, that all are small and that none of them takes more than fifteen minutes to pass from the Ormeau Bridge to Donegall Pass.

Loyalists in the Donegall Pass area formed their own group ACORD (A Community Response to Despotism), to protest at republican parades that cross the bottom of the Pass and to support the right of 'traditional protestant cultural parades' to use the lower Ormeau Road. Two parades were re-routed and ACORD also blocked the Ormeau Road and disrupted traffic on a number of occasions in protest at the stopping of Orange parades. ACORD point out that the lower Ormeau has been defined as a nationalist area by LOCC. They point out that many of the Orangemen based in Ballynafeigh once lived in the lower Ormeau area, which in reality still includes a substantial loyalist community in the Donegall Pass area, whose feelings are largely ignored in the debate. They also note that no opposition to the parades has been expressed by residents in the Holy Land or University Street areas and these people have been excluded from the debate as they are not regarded as a part of either community. In reality then they say that the lower Ormeau area - from the Ormeau Bridge to the Pass and on both sides of the road - is a much more diverse community than LOCC acknowledge. Another loyalist group, ORDER (Ormeau Residents Demand Equal Rights), is based in the Ballynafeigh area and is campaigning specifically for loyal order parades to be allowed down the Ormeau Road.

Members of the loyal orders also claim that the residents group is not representative and speaks for only a small number of those living in the area, this is illustrated by the large number of outsiders who have helped to swell their protests. The LOCC have responded by stating that they canvassed opinion extensively in the area and have held public meetings to put over their arguments. They also note that the Orangemen represent no-one but themselves and that many of those on the Orange parades do not come from Ballynafeigh.

BELFAST, Springfield Road: Nationalist residents on the Springfield Road object to a mini-Twelfth parade that crosses the peace line at Ainsworth Avenue to walk to the Whiterock Orange Hall. Nationalists say that many people were killed in the area during the Troubles, that there has often been trouble in the past at this parade and that changes to the route had been enforced on more than one occasion. They object to the idea that the Orange Order could demand to walk through nationalist areas and to the scale of the policing that was necessary to secure the route.

Orangemen responded by stating that it only takes a few minutes to parade along the Springfield Road, that there are few houses in the area in question, while further up the road the houses are mixed, and it is the most direct way of walking to the Orange Hall. Supporters of the paramilitary groups have said that the parade should be allowed to continue and they would ensure that no unruly elements from the Shankill area would be allowed to get near to the nationalist area.

BELFAST, Suffolk: loyalist residents raised objections to two republican parades that pass the top of Black's Road on the way from Twinbrook to the Falls Road. Republicans stated that the parades had always passed peacefully and there had never been any protests from the residents of the Suffolk estate in previous years. The first parade was blocked by the police, the second was voluntarily re-routed.

BELLAGHY has a population of 1,041, and is estimated by residents to be 80% nationalist. A residents group - Bellaghy Concerned Residents - was formed in Spring 1995 to campaign against loyalist parades in the village and the extensive policing that accompanies them. In particular the group object to the mini-Twelfth parade in early July which draws 30 or more bands to Bellaghy and dominates the entire village for the evening. The residents complained that they feel intimidated during the parade and that despite the scale of the policing nothing is done to stop excessive drinking and urinating in public. They also objected to the loyalists parading into nationalist estates on the morning of the Twelfth and the Last Saturday parades. The group acknowledge that a number of the Orangemen live in the village but also argue that many of them do not. They feel that the band parade in particular is intrusive by attracting hundreds of loyalists from a wide area into Bellaghy, while no consideration is given to the feelings of the majority of the residents. The group said that they gathered a petition opposing the parades which was signed by a large percentage of the villagers and presented it to the local RUC, but it was ignored.

CASTLEDERG has a population of 2,579, which is evenly divided between the two communities. Loyalists objected to republican groups parading into the centre of Castlederg, which they say was the most bombed town in Northern Ireland during the Troubles. The first republican parade was stopped in the Ferguson Crescent area, the second one was permitted to enter the Diamond for a rally. The week after the first republican parade there was trouble at a loyalist band parade. This parade had followed the same route for 19 years without causing problems. Last year trouble began when a tricolour was removed from a lamppost at Ferguson Crescent. There was also trouble in late August when rioting broke out several hours after the Last Saturday Black parade had been held in the town. It has been suggested that although the parade had been adequately policed, too few officers remained to control late night drinkers.

Republicans point out that there are numerous loyalist parades in the town throughout the marching season, including many late at night. They say that they are not trying to stop these parades but simply want the right to parade in the centre of their own town if they so desire. It was suggested that having achieved their aim of holding a parade and rally in the centre of the town, the nationalists had made their point. It did not necessarily mean that they would apply for similar parades in the future.

Loyalists were angered when the republican parade was allowed into the town centre because of the past history of IRA violence and they say that it left a lot of ill-feeling. They say that the band parade followed a well established route to an outlying estate with a large Protestant population. Band members claim that their parade was attacked by bystanders who were hanging around a pub and it was in response to the loyalist protests at the republican parade.

DERRY. The parent clubs of the Apprentice Boys of Derry have traditionally paraded around the walls of the city on the morning of the Relief of Derry parade on August 12. Between 1970 and 1995 the walls were closed and no parades were allowed, although the Apprentice Boys formerly requested permission to walk the traditional route each year. In 1995 the circuit of the walls was reopened and the police gave permission for the Apprentice Boys to parade.

Local people formed the Bogside Residents Group to oppose the resumption of the parade of the complete circuit of the walls. They have no objections to the Apprentice Boys parading in the city or on parts of the walls that do not overlook the nationalist areas but they should not parade along the section of the walls that overlook the Bogside. They state that before the Troubles, coins and verbal abuse were regularly hurled from the walls into the Bogside during the parade. Last August they offered to discuss their objections to the parade with the Apprentice Boys but the Boys refused to meet them. On the morning of the parade there was an attempt to resolve the protest when the RUC presented some compromise proposals but these were unacceptable to the protesters. They also criticised the police handling of the protest.

The Apprentice Boys argue that the parade has been a central part of their tradition for more than 200 years. They say that the parade takes place at 9.30 on a Saturday morning when few people are about, that the parade can barely be seen from the Bogside area and that the nearest residents are a hundred yards away. Furthermore the parade begins outside the headquarters of the Apprentice Boys, it takes less than half an hour to complete the entire circuit and only a few minutes to pass by the contentious area. Above all they claim it is a dignified procession to church.

They also noted that they offered a number of concessions to the police some of which they imposed on themselves: they would reduce the number of bands, no music would be played over the disputed section of the walls, only members of the Parent Clubs would walk the walls and no 'hangers-on' would be allowed onto the walls. They also offered to allow the protesters to remain on the walls while they walked passed. They acknowledged that there was some trouble as the parade passed through the Diamond later in the day but claimed it had been exaggerated by the media and most of the damage was caused by republicans rioting against the police. Officers of the Apprentice Boys felt the parade passed successfully and they were pleased with the dignity and discipline of their members; they say that concessions they offered showed that they had been willing to compromise but the nationalists had not been interested.

DOWNPATRICK has a population of 10,113 and a nationalist majority. A local band, the Red Hand Defenders, want to hold their annual parade through the predominately Protestant and commercial Church Street and Bridge Street areas of the town. The parade was permitted in 1982 but it ended in violent clashes between Catholics and Protestants. Since then the parade has been banned from the centre of town. The band cancelled the parade for four years from 1990 in the hope that this would be seen as a gesture of compromise but it did not have any effect. They also offered to consider alternative routes but the RUC will not allow them to parade the town. In September 1995 the parade was marred by visiting bands and their supporters attacking the police. The Red Hand Defenders are not optimistic that they will be able to parade in their own town in the near future but they will keep trying. Band members say that nationalist groups parade through the town and that Orange Order are allowed through the town on the Twelfth and therefore they too should be permitted to parade.

LURGAN. Republicans want the right to march into the centre of Lurgan, a town of 21,905 people, evenly divided between the two communities. Two parades were re-routed in 1995 and two unofficial protests were broken up by police. A third parade was stopped in March 1996. Loyalist protesters claim that republicans have never held traditional marches in the town centre and they further justified their opposition by pointing out that the town centre had only just been rebuilt following a large IRA bomb in 1992.

Republicans point to the numerous loyalist parades through the town centre. They say that many of these pass near to a nationalist estate and these parades frequently disrupt their access to the town. In contrast they are never allowed near the town centre. Parades organised by the Hibernians and Foresters and the Easter Commemoration parade are all allowed to pass behind the church from Edward Street to North Street but no nationalist parades are allowed into the main commercial area. The Nationalist Right to March Group state that they are not protesting against loyalist parades in the town, but simply demanding the same rights. They say all their parades are held on a Sunday afternoon when the town is deserted and would therefore not cause any disruption; instead loyalists are going out of their way to be offended and the massive police presence is an unnecessary waste of money.

PORTADOWN has a population of 21,299 of which about 70% are Protestant. The majority of Catholics live in the Obins Street and Garvaghy Road areas. Until 1985 three loyalist parades passed through the nearby Obins Street area, but following protests by residents these were re-routed by the police to enter the town by the Garvaghy Road. The Garvaghy Road Residents Group was formed in Spring 1995 to campaign to have Orange parades re-routed away from the area.

Residents object to any loyalist parades along the road and say the Orangemen should respect their wishes and use an alternative route away from nationalist areas. They claim that there is no need for the parade to go down the Garvaghy Road after the Drumcree church service and instead it should return they way it came, which avoids the nationalist areas. While they agree that in an ideal world everyone should be able to walk where they wish, they say that nationalists already feel second class citizens in their own town. They point out that while there are frequent Orange parades in the centre of Portadown throughout the marching season, nationalist parades are never allowed outside nationalist areas.

The Portadown Orangemen say that they have paraded to and from Drumcree Church since 1809, and Obins Street is the traditional route for country lodges to enter town on the morning of the Twelfth. They say that when their parades began there were no nationalist estates only fields, and even today the houses are well set back from the road and few properties face onto the road itself. They claim that the Residents Group is not representative of the people who live in the area, they have not been elected in any way and are not interested in compromise. The Orangemen insist that they do not intend to cause offence, that the main parade along the route is a church parade at which only hymns or noncontroversial tunes are played and that the parade would take only 15 minutes to pass. They ask that the residents respect their traditions.

OTHERS. Besides the organised protests at parades in the above mentioned towns there were also minor problems at a number of other locations. In particular those at the Short Strand in Belfast and at Dunloy, Pomeroy, Rosslea and Rasharkin have potential to become more significant in the future. In each of these cases the problem was one of loyalist parades being held in predominately nationalist areas. At the same time as many parades are held on a rotating cycle of more than a year, future marching season may throw up protests in yet more places.

SECTION 14: REVIEW OF MAIN ISSUES

There are now over 3000 parades in Northern Ireland annually the vast majority of which are held by 'loyalist' groups and institutions. Although most of these parades are not directly disputed the sheer number and frequency of parades does cause resentment amongst sections of both the Catholic and Protestant communities. More significantly, those parades that are disputed have serious consequences for community relations within Northern Ireland.

Why are there such a large number of parades and why does the number appear to be increasing?
1. Parades and demonstrations, which have been common throughout western Europe, have remained particularly important in Northern Ireland due to ongoing ethnic differences which are highlighted in a lack of agreement over the nature of the state. Particular types of parades are understood as part of a communities 'tradition' distinguishing it from the other community.
2. The historical position of the Orange Institution in the north of Ireland, and within Northern Ireland since 1921, has provided the environment in which loyalist parades could flourish whereas nationalist and republican parades have been restricted to particular areas. In other words, the 'tradition' of parading has been largely based on an inequality of power.
3. The number of loyalist parades may has risen because of the divisions within Unionism and the insecurities brought about by 'the Troubles'. Splits within unionism has left the Orange Institution, which is still directly tied to the Ulster Unionist Party, as less representative of diverse unionist politics. This has led to an increase in the number of local parades many of which are held by other groups particularly marching bands. Whilst parading remains an important part of unionist political culture it is no longer the expression of unity that it previously might have been. In a state in which the Orange Institution is politically less powerful loyalist parades have become more diverse and more localised.
4. Increased political confidence within the nationalist community has led both to an increase in the number of parades particularly by republican groups. Given the prolonged IRA campaign many of these parades are seen as threatening within the Protestant community.
5. Parades continue to be used by politicians and political groups for

their short term political ends.

What effect have these changes had upon parading in Northern Ireland?

1. Years of sectarian violence and tensions within Northern Ireland has reduced the acceptability of loyalist parades to many in the nationalist community and probably an increasing, although less vocal, proportion of the Protestant community. The parades have become 'less respectable'.
2. The increase in the number of blood and thunder bands and the more disparate nature of unionist politics has reduced the authority that senior Orangemen appear to have over the events they are organising. The Orange Institution no longer represents, and therefore has less authority over, the majority of those involved in parades.
3. The sheer number of parades, particularly in predominantly Protestant towns, appears to have increased the alienation that the Catholic community feel toward the civic centres of those towns.
4. Residents groups in some nationalist areas have become more confident in expressing opposition to loyalist parades, particularly after the IRA and loyalist paramilitary ceasefires.
5. The parades have, more than ever, come to define the communal boundaries in Northern Ireland.
6. The parading issue has proved detrimental to the relationship the RUC have with both Catholic and Protestant communities despite efforts by the police to improve their position as a police force for all the communities. Since they most often try to maintain the status quo they are perceived by nationalist, and with some justification, as sustaining the imbalances that exist in public political expression which date back to the Stormont era. On the other hand, if they attempt to reduce or reroute parades, as they have done in some areas, they are inevitably accused of attacking the 'tradition' and the 'rights' of the Protestant community.

Approaches to resolution

This report discusses a number of options that have been raised as a means of resolving the problem of disputed parades. Some of these could be acted on in the short term others would need longer term planning and implementation. These are not recommendations but proposals for discussion.
1. Negotiation and Mediation
At present disputes over the right to parade are either resolved by the police making decisions according to the Public Order (NI) Order 1987,

and physically enforcing that decision if necessary, or through intermediaries mediating an agreement or some accommodation between interested parties. Whilst both methods might produce short term answers in particular instances they are unlikely to prove effective in improving the general environment in which public political expression in Northern Ireland takes place. Consequently the problem of the right to parade remains as a blight upon community relations.

Four points appear to be clear:
i. In principle everyone should have the right to parade as an expression of their cultural identity.
ii. The right to parade must be balanced by the rights of residents through which proposed parades might pass.
iii. Those organising parades need to held accountable and responsible for the totality of what takes place.
iv. Some method needs to be found within which arbitration and adjudication of disputes can take place.

A number of proposals which may move towards an improvement in the situation might be considered.

2. A Parading Commission

A commission could be set up in the short term which might develop a set of principles under which political expression in Northern Ireland could take place. In particular, accommodation might be found between the rights of communities not to be disturbed by parades and the rights of others to hold parades. These principles should be developed around ideas of consensus and accommodation rather than consent and tradition. The Commission could also offer an overview of all the disputed parades and make recommendations which would treat all parade disputes as a single issue. The Commission would work to a specific brief and be asked to make recommendations within a short period of time. Its role would be advisory.

3. Use of the Law

Consideration should be given to whether all sections of the Public Order (NI) Order 1987 are being fully utilised, or to whether further legislation is required to improve the control of parades and demonstrations.

4. Responsible Parading

Consideration should be given to the introduction of measures by those organising and those policing parades which enforce upon participants a greater responsibility for the events.

i. *General Behaviour*: The organisers of parades could take greater responsibility, and be seen to be taking greater responsibility, for what takes place in the events they organise. There are a whole series of areas which might be considered:
    * Better publicity of when and where parades are taking place.
    * Better liaison with local community groups.
    * Better control of sectarian music and chanting.
    * Improved controls on the displays of sectarian symbols.
    * The possibility that flags might be furled or music stopped in particular areas.
    * The avoidance of Catholic churches on parade routes.
    * Restricting access to parts of a route to the parade only.

ii. *Stewarding and Marshaling* - The role of parade stewards should be considered. What exactly should be their role? Should they liaise with community representatives? Are they clearly visible and distinct from the parade? Do they have adequate training?

iii. *Community Liaison* - Greater efforts might be made by parade organisers to liaise with representatives of the communities through which the parade will pass.

iv. *Voluntary re-routing* - Organisers might take into consideration local sensitivities towards parades and consider a moratorium on events in an area over a specified time period.

v. *Externally Imposed Constraints* - Consideration might be given to an advisory body or commission that could oversee public political expression in Northern Ireland (see below).

vi. *Financial Constraints* - Users of public spaces such as motorists, building contractors and race organisers have to cover themselves for financial liability. Consideration might be given to organisers of parades being required either to put down a financial bond or take out liability insurance against damage or violent behaviour during the parade.

5. A Parading Tribunal

A tribunal to consider parades could take a number or combination of forms:
  i. A mediator or 'watchdog'.
  ii. An arbitrator on particular disputes.
  iii. A series of locally formed committees empowered to make judgements on specific local disputes.

6. Parade 'Planning' Permission

A commission to which all applications to parade should be made months in advance and which would adjudicate on contested applications. This would require significant revision to public order legislation.

A system set up to consider parading disputes has a number of advantages:

  i. It would reduce the role of the police in 'arbitrating' parade disputes.
  ii. It would introduce some consistency to the decisions made over different parades.
  iii. It would be able to make judgements on a wider set of criteria than simply public order.
  iv. It would allow the public imposition of 'conditions' in particular instances.
  v. It would make the decision making process more public and more accountable.
  vi. It would allow both communities to use the force of argument and not the force of numbers.
  vii. It could guarantee both the rights of those that wish to parade and the rights of residents.

However there are a number of problems with such a proposal:

  * It would be difficult to find a structure within which the tribunal could work which would be seen as legitimate by all those within the parading disputes.

* It would, in all probability, require major revision to current public order legislation.
* It would significantly increase the bureaucracy surrounding applications to demonstrate, although the cost of this could easily be offset if it served to reduce the required policing of events.

Most parades are peaceful and cause little or no offence. In the majority of cases the behaviour and discipline is perfectly acceptable. But methods need to be found to resolve the problems that do exist so that parades no longer damage community relations. The long term aim should not be to prevent parades from taking place but rather to encourage a political environment where civil rights are respected and political expression can take place without threatening or inconveniencing the lives of others.

REFERENCES

Bardon, J. (1992) *A History of Ulster.* Belfast, Blackstaff Press.
Bell, D. (1990) *Acts of Union: Youth and Sectarian Culture in Northern Ireland.* London, Macmillan Press.
Bew, P, Gibbon, P. and Patterson, H. (1995) *Northern Ireland 1921-1994. Political Forces and Social Classes.* London, Serif.
Boal, F. (1995) *Shaping a City. Belfast in the late Twentieth Century.* Belfast, Institute of Irish Studies.
Boyle J. W. (1962-63) 'The Belfast Protestant Association and the Independent Orange Order, 1901-10' *Irish Historical Studies,* Vol. XIII, pp 117-152.
Bruce, S. (1986) *God Save Ulster. The Religion and Politics of Paisleyism.* Oxford, OUP.
Bruce, S. (1992) *The Red Hand. Protestant Paramilitaries in Northern Ireland.* Oxford, OUP.
Bryan, D. (1994) 'Interpreting the Twelfth'. *History Ireland,* Vol. 2, No. 2.
Bryan, D, Fraser, T. and Dunn, S. (1995) *Political Rituals. Loyalist Parades in Portadown.* Coleraine, Centre for the Study of Conflict.
Bryan, D. and Officer, D. (1995) 'The Framework Document and the Politics of Symbolism' Salford, *European Consortium for Political Research Review,* Salford University.
Bryan, D. and Tonkin, E. (in press) 'Political Ritual: Time and Temporality' in *Political Ritual* ed. Görun Aijmer & Asa Boholm, Gothenburg, Institute for Advanced Studies in Social Anthropology, Gothenburg University.
Bryson, L. and McCartney, C. (1994) *Clashing Symbols: a report on the use of flags, anthems and other national symbols in Northern Ireland.* Belfast, Institute of Irish Studies.
Buckley, A. (1985-86) 'The Chosen Few': Biblical Texts in the Regalia of an Ulster Secret Society. *Folk Life,* Volume 29.
Buckley, A. and M. Kenney (1995) *Negotiating Identity. Rhetoric, Metaphor and Social Drama in Northern Ireland.* Washington, Smithsonian Institute Press.
Cohen, A. (1993) *Masquerade Politics.* Oxford, Berg Publications.
Dewar, M, Brown, J. and Long, S. (1967) *Orangeism: a new historical appreciation.* Belfast, Grand Orange Lodge of Ireland.

Fair Employment Commission. (1996) *Annual Report*. Belfast, FEC.
Giulianotti, R., Bonney, N. and Hepworth, M. (eds) (1994) *Football, Violence and Social Identity*. London, Routledge.
Hanlon, K. (1994) *Community Relations in Ballynafeigh. A study of attitudes to community relations in a mixed area of Belfast*. Belfast, Ballynafeigh Community Development Association.
Harbinson, J. (1973) *The Ulster Unionist Party 1882-1973: Its Development and Organisation*. Belfast, Blackstaff Press.
Jarman, N. (1992) 'Troubled Images. The Iconography of Loyalism'. *Critique of Anthropology*, Vol. 12, No 2.
Jarman, N. (1993) *Intersecting Belfast*. in B. Bender (ed) *Landscape: Politics and Perspectives*. Oxford, Berg Publications.
Jarman, N. (1995) *Parading Culture. Parades and Visual Displays in Northern Ireland*. Unpublished PhD Thesis, University College London.
Jarman, N. (in press) *The Phoenix and the Sash. Commemorating 1916 in Belfast,* in A. Forty and S. Kuechler (eds) *Monuments and Memory*. Oxford, Berg Publications.
Jones, R., Kane, J. S., Wallace, R., Sloan, D., Courtney, B. (1996) *Orange Citadel. A History of Orangeism in Portadown*. Portadown, Portadown Orange Lodge District No. 1.
Hepburn, A. C. (1990) 'The Belfast Riots of 1935'. *Social History*, Vol. XV.
Kennedy, B. (ed) (1990) *A Celebration: 1690-1990, The Orange Institution*. Belfast, Grand Orange Lodge of Ireland.
Kennedy, B. (ed) (1995) *Steadfast for Faith and Freedom: 200 Years of Orangeism*. Belfast, Grand Orange Lodge of Ireland.
McCann, E. (1980) *War and an Irish Town*. London, Pluto Press.
McClelland, A. (1968) 'The origin of the Imperial Grand Black Chapter of the British Commonwealth'. *Royal Society of Antiquaries of Ireland*, Volume 98.
Moloney, E. and Pollock, A. (1986) *Paisley*. Dublin, Poolbeg Press.
Montgomery, G. and Whitten, J. (1995) *The Order on Parade*. Belfast, GOLI Education Committee.
Morgan, A. (1991) *Labour and Partition: The Belfast Working Class 1905-23*. London, Pluto Press.
Murdie, W., Cargo, D., Kilpatrick, C. (nd) *History of the Royal Arch Purple*. The Royal Arch Purple Research Group.

O'Connor, F. (1993) *In Search of a State. Catholics in Northern Ireland.* Belfast, Blackstaff Press.

O'Dowd, L. (1993) *Craigavon: Locality, economy and the State in a Failed 'New City'.* In C. Curtin, H. Donnan and T. Wilson (eds) *Irish Urban Cultures.* Belfast, Institute of Irish Studies.

Pat Finucane Centre (1995) *One Day in August.* Derry, Pat Finucane Centre.

Patterson, H. (1980) *Class Conflict and Sectarianism: The Protestant Working Class and the Belfast Labour Movement, 1868-1920.* Belfast, Blackstaff Press.

Purdie, B. (1990) Politics in the Streets. *The Origins of the Civil Rights Movement in Northern Ireland.* Belfast, Blackstaff Press.

Sheehan, M. (1995) 'Fair Employment: an issue for the peace process'. *Race and Class*, Vol. 37, No 1.

Tercentenary Committee (1988) Official Brochure of the Tercentenary Celebrations of the Apprentice Boys of Derry Association. Londonderry.

Wright, Frank (1987) *Northern Ireland: A Comparative Analysis.* Dublin, Gill and Macmillan.

Wright, Frank (1996) *Two Lands on One Soil: Ulster Politics Before Home Rule.* Dublin, Gill and Macmillan.

CENTRE FOR THE STUDY OF CONFLICT

PUBLICATIONS LIST

1996 PUBLICATIONS

'Inter-Faith Marriages in Northern Ireland' by Grace Fraser, Valerie Morgan, Gillian Robinson and Marie Smith, 60 pages, £4.
    This new report on Mixed Marriages in Northern Ireland looks closely at the whole range of past research findings on this subject and then sets out to investigate the social and institutional context within which mixed (or inter-faith) marriage exist and survive in Northern Ireland. In particular the problems and difficulties created for mixed couples with regard to religion, education and housing are examined and discussed in this report.

'Ethnic Residential Segregation in Belfast' by Michael A. Poole and Paul Doherty (1996), 290 pages, available May (about £12).
    This is the second of a two volume monograph on ethnic residential segregation in Northern Ireland. This first volume dealt with Belfast (see 1995 list below); this second volume deal swith the rest of the province. The authors have collected data on residential segregation for many years and much of the material presented here is new or reanalysed.

'Education for Mutual Understanding: the Statutory Years' by Alan Smith and Alan Robinson, 100 pages, available May (about £5).
    This is the final report of a three-year research and evaluation project which concentrated on the introduction of a cross-curricular theme, Education for Mutual Understanding (EMU), to the school curriculum in Northern Ireland. It follows on from a previous report *EMU: Perceptions and Policy*, (see 1992 list below). It is based on work with teachers in a number of schools to see what approaches seem most fruitful in introducing EMU into the whole school environment. It then worked with a cross section of people within the overall education system who are involved in the implementation of EMU. This final report represents an insight into the development of EMU within schools as part of the curriculum during the initial statutory years (1992-95).

In preparation:

'Community Development' by Sam McCready.

'Ethnic Minorities in Northern Ireland' by Greg Irwin

1995 PUBLICATIONS

'A Framework for the North?' by Keith Kyle (1995), 15 pages, £1.50. (ISBN 1-85923-0172)
> In this short paper the distinguished journalist and commentator Keith Kyle makes an analysis of the Documents 'Frameworks for the Future on Northern Ireland' published in February 1995. He argues that, despite general unionist opposition to them, their most likely effect will be to ensure the continuation of partition in Ireland for the foreseeable future.

'Political Rituals: Loyalist Parades in Portadown' by Dominic Bryan, T. G. Fraser and Seamus Dunn (1995), 74 pages, £4.00. (ISBN 1-85923-002-4)
> The ever-topical subject of parades and marches in Northern Ireland has received surprisingly little academic analysis based on field research. This carefully focused and detailed study looks at the recent history of controversial parades in Portadown, based on a careful perusal of relevant documentation along with interviews with a wide range of involved individuals and groups. Many of the more general issues are of necessity raised and discussed.

'Majority Minority Review 1: Education in a Divided Society (Second Edition)' by A. M. Gallagher (1995), 81 pages, £4.00. (ISBN 1-85923-003-2)
> The first edition of this carefully organised assembly of data and analysis on the two main educational systems in Northern Ireland was published in 1989. It immediately sold out, and has been reprinted many times since. This is a completely new edition, updated to take account of new data both from official sources and from more recent researches. It is an invaluable repository of information on the educational system of Northern Ireland and has great relevance for those studying education in divided societies generally.

'Sport and Community Relations in Northern Ireland' by John Sugden and Scott Harvie (1995), 92 pages, £5.00. (ISBN 1-85923-091-1)

The work of John Sugden and his colleagues on the often vexing and divisive matter of sport in divided communities is well-known both in Ireland and internationally. This paper reports on a an innovative and ground-breaking survey which collects and analyses data about a range of aspects of the role of sport within Northern Ireland with respect both to community coherence and community separation and division.

'Policing a Divided Society' by Andrew Hamilton, Linda Moore and Tim Trimble (1995), 157 pages, £8.00. (ISBN 1-85923-027 X)

The peace process in Northern Ireland has allowed the spotlight to be focused on a number of important social and political issues which the violence had obscured or made difficult to discuss. One of the most central and controversial questions relates to the future of policing in Northern Ireland. The research reported here is based on detailed and comprehensive field work over two years in three locations in Northern Ireland. It examines the history of policing, how it is legally and administratively structured, and identifies the most salient issues. It then collects and analyses the perceptions of communities, their political and community representatives, and police-related individuals and organisations with respect to the complete range of contested issues. It ends by making a number of recommendations arising out of the data and its analysis.

'The Quaker Peace Education Project 1988-1994: Developing Untried Strategies' by Jerry Tyrrell (1995), 122 pages, £5.00 (ISBN 1-85923-007-5)

The Quaker Peace Education Project was established at Magee College in Derry in 1988. It was initiated by the late Professor Andrew Young and received considerable material and moral support from the Quaker community throughout its six-year life. This exhaustive report, written by the project's first and only director, describes the history and development of the work of the project, its practice and its theoretical supports. It also presents a close and detailed description and analysis of the project's development work in schools and in a range of community organisations.

'Peer Mediation in Primary Schools' by Jerry Tyrrell and Seamus Farrell (1995), 83 pages, £5.00. (ISBN 1-85923-004-0)
> This report describes an experiment in the development and use of peer mediation techniques in a number of primary schools in Northern Ireland. It analyses the series of steps involved in developing the programme, the difficulties experienced and the mistakes made. Finally the report reaches a number of conclusions and makes recommendations about future developments.

'Occasional Paper Number 3: What's Wrong with Conflict?' by J. Darby (1995, 1991), 14 pages, £1.50. (ISBN 1-85923-096-2)
> This Occasional Paper was first printed in 1991 and has been in constant demand ever since. This is a second (unrevised) printing.

'Disability and Religion in Northern Ireland' by Martin Melaugh (1995), 56 pages, £5.00. (ISBN 1 85923 046 6)
> This report was published earlier this year.

'Ethnic Residential Segregation in Belfast' by Paul Doherty and Michael A. Poole (1995), 110 pages, £6.00. (ISBN 1 85923 023 7)
> This is the first of a two volume monograph on ethnic residential segregation in Northern Ireland. This first volume deals with Belfast; the second - published in 1996 - deals with the rest of the province. The authors have collected data on residential segregation for many years and much of the material presented here is new or reanalysed.

1994 PUBLICATIONS

'The Emu Promoting School - a Report on a Conference on Education for Mutual Understanding and Cultural Heritage' by Alan Smith (1994), £2.00. (ISBN 1 85923 095 4)

'The Company we Keep: Women Community and Organisations' by V. Morgan and G. Fraser (1994), £5.00. (ISBN 1 85923 065 2)

'A Welling up of Deep Unconscious Forces: Psychology and the Northern Ireland Conflict' by Ed Cairns (1994) £4.00. (ISBN 1 85923 070 9)

'Community Relations and Local Government' by C. Knox, J. Hughes, D. Birrell And S. McCready (1994) £8.00. (ISBN 1 85923 060 1)

'Majority Minority Review Number 3: Housing and Religion in Northern Ireland' by Martin Melaugh (1994) £5.00. (ISBN 1 85923 046 6)
'Protestant Alienation in Northern Ireland' by S. Dunn and V. Morgan (1994) £4.00. (ISBN 1 85923 075 X)

'The Churches and Inter-Community Relationships' by D. Morrow, D. Birrell, J. Greer and T. O'Keeffe (1991, 1994) £10.
(ISBN 1 87 1206 07 3)

'The Promise of Evaluation: What Evaluation Offers Policymakers and Practitioners', by Clem McCartney (1992, 1994) £1.00.
(ISBN 1 871206 13 8)

1993 PUBLICATIONS

'The Chance of a Lifetime an Evaluation of Project Children' by Alan Smith and Dominic Murray (1993) £3.00. (ISBN 1 871206 49 9)

'Register of Research on Northern Ireland' by C. Ó Maoláin (1993) £5.00.
(ISBN 1 871206 69 3)

'Breaking the Mould: the Roles of Parents and Teachers in the Integrated Schools in Northern Ireland' by V. Morgan, S. Dunn, E. Cairns and G. Fraser (1992) £3.00. (ISBN 1 871206 43x)

'Occasional Paper Number 5: The Common School' by Seamus Dunn (1993) £3.00. (ISBN 1 871206 89 8)

1992 and pre-1992 PUBLICATIONS

'Education for Mutual Understanding - Perceptions and Policy' by A. Smith and A. Robinson (1992), £3.00. (ISBN 1 871206 38 3)

'Majority Minority Review 2: Employment, Unemployment and Religion in Northern Ireland' by A. M. Gallagher (1991), £5.95.
(ISBN 1 871206 17 0)

'Occasional Paper Number 4: Comparative Approaches to Community Relations' edited by J. Darby and A. M. Gallagher (1991), £2.50.
(ISBN 1 871206 87 1)

'Peace Building in a Political Impasse: Cross-Border Links In Ireland' by D. Murray and J. O'Neill (1991), £3.00. (ISBN 1 871206 12x)

'Comparative Approaches To Community Relations' edited by J. Darby and A. M. Gallagher (1991), £2.50. (ISBN 1 871206 87 1)
'Extending School Links' by A. Smith and S. Dunn (1990), £3.50. (ISBN 1 871206 86 3)

Occasional Paper Number 2: Conflict Research' by M. Hayes (1990), £1.50.

'Education and Community in Northern Ireland: Schools Apart?' and 'Schools Together?' by J. Darby, D. Murray, D. Batts, S. Dunn, S. Farren and J. Harris, and by S. Dunn, J. Darby and K. Mullan (1977 and 1984: reprinted in one volume, 1989), £5.00. (ISBN 1 871206 91 X)

'Integrated Schools: Information for Parents' by D. Wilson And S. Dunn (1989), £1.95. (ISBN 1 87 1206 367)

'Employment In Divided Societies' edited by A. C. Hepburn (1981), £2.00. (ISBN 901229 42 3)

Copies of the above Reports are available in Bookshops or, by Post, from:

Ruth McIlwaine
The Centre for the Study of Conflict
University of Ulster, Cromore Road
Coleraine
Northern Ireland, BT52 1SA

Tel: (01265) - 324666 or (01265) - 324165
Fax: (01265) - 324917.